To Janice,

Blessings to you!

ADVENTURES
IN THE
PROPHETIC

ADVENTURES
IN THE
PROPHETIC

JAMES W. GOLL, MICHAL ANN GOLL,
MICKEY ROBINSON, JEFF JANSEN,
RYAN WYATT, AND PATRICIA KING

DESTINY IMAGE® PUBLISHERS, INC.
P.O. Box 310, Shippensburg, PA 17257-0310

"Speaking to the Purposes of God for this Generation and for the Generations to Come."

This book and all other Destiny Image, Revival Press, MercyPlace, Fresh Bread, Destiny Image Fiction, and Treasure House books are available at Christian bookstores and distributors worldwide.

For a U.S. bookstore nearest you, call **1-800-722-6774.**

For more information on foreign distributors, call **717-532-3040.**

Reach us on the Internet: **www.destinyimage.com.**

ISBN 10: 0-7684-3163-8

ISBN 13: 978-0-7684-3163-6

For Worldwide Distribution, Printed in the U.S.A.

1 2 3 4 5 6 7 8 9 10 11 / 14 13 12 11 10

CONTENTS

Preface

Cultivating an Adventure Streak

My mom always told me I was the most curious of her three kids. I think that helps explain the fact that I was the one who always got bored the easiest, too! I never seem to have lost that trait from my early childhood. I love a great adventure! Don't you? I just hate to be bored.

Now it may take me awhile to warm up to the unknown, but give me some adjustment time, and I will take the plunge. One of my fondest recent experiences was when my four young adult kids and I went off-road four-wheeling in the beautiful desert near Sedona, Arizona. I was really uncertain for awhile (quite awhile, actually). I rode uncomfortably on the back with one of my daughters driving, eating dust and holding on for dear life. Then I had had enough of backseat driving. I wanted an adventure myself. Dude! That is exactly what I got! I took the wheel and wow, I had the time of my life blasting across the landscape. Even my kids were impressed.

What a wide vista of experience is on the other side of the safe and familiar path. To have an adventure, you must break through an invisible membrane of the familiar into someplace that previously made you uncomfortable. You pass through constraints constructed in your past and you carve a path for your future.

Adventure (noun)—an unusual and exciting, typically hazardous, experience or activity. A daring and exciting activity calling for enthusiasm. *Adventure* (verb)—to engage in hazardous and exciting activity, especially the exploration of unknown territory. Now that sounds like something I signed up for! I want my whole life to be a series of adventures in the Kingdom of God.

Once I had a vivid dream in which the Holy Spirit brought me to a door. I was uncertain about whether or not to go through the door because I felt that I would be uncomfortable with whatever was on the other side. In the dream, I simply touched the door and it opened right up, like stepping onto an automatic door opener in front of a department store. I gazed through the doorway, and I saw a hallway, like one in a school or hospital, lined with many other doors. I leaned in. The voice of the Holy Spirit spoke in my inner being and said, "I am leading you to a door that will lead to other doors." I knew that behind each one of these other new doors was a fresh, creative adventure. That sounded like a sure cure for boredom to me!

I awoke from the dream knowing that if I would tackle the fear of going through that first doorway, I could enter into a lifetime of adventures greater than I ever could have imagined. The first door I had to press through was fear. Fear of man. Fear of rejection. Fear of the unknown. Fear of fear. I knew that if I would press past my own personal fears, I would be able to open a door in the Spirit for others to follow.

That is what has happened. My late wife, Michal Ann, often used to wear a black "No Fear" baseball cap when she ministered. On the inside of the rim of the cap it read, "Don't let your fears stand in the way of your dreams." Yes, that is it! Push past your fears so you, too, can live an adventurous life.

THE ADVENTURE COMPANY

You see, I have been dreaming about this particular book, *Adventures in the Prophetic,* for a long time. I have wanted to assemble an "Adventure

Company"—people who are not necessarily the greatest platform preachers of history, not necessarily the richest people in the world, but definitely a group who will venture forth without hesitation into dark places to take new territory for the King of kings. This Adventure Company is full of curiosity. They will risk their reputations so that Jesus' light can shine. Together, their voices will introduce you to the amazing diversity of prophetic adventures that you, too, can encounter.

My prophetic friends and I will inspire you with testimonies and ground you in the Word of God. First, I will bring some of my vintage teaching on the power and the perils of the prophetic to help you push through that first door. Then we will turn to one of my best friends and one of the planet's craziest believers, Mickey Robinson. He is going to impart spiritual bravery and provide you with a foundation of how to properly receive prophetic ministry from a fellow believer.

Then we start down our hallway and start looking behind some of the other doors. Patricia King, founder of Extreme Prophetic, will open the door to The Prophetic and Justice. (Is that one ever a word from the Lord!) Jeff Jansen, leader of Global Fire Ministries, will take you into a room filled with the revelatory and glory realms of God. Then you will go through a doorway into a room where my wife dwelled—the convergence of intercessory prayer and the prophetic. I am honored to bring her timeless lessons to you.

Continuing down the hallway, you will peer behind some other doors into rooms that explain some of the purposes of the prophetic in our day. Ryan Wyatt of Abiding Glory Ministries, another rising, next-generation leader, will paint a picture of the power of the prophetic to bring Heaven to earth. As two of the fathers of the prophetic movement, Mickey and I will close things out with a glint in our eyes toward the future. Yes, the prophetic supplies us with the power to outwit the enemy so that we can enter into the coming great harvest!

Sound interesting? No, it is more than that—it is exciting! This will be an Adventure in the Prophetic! Come on in!

With eager expectation,

—James W. Goll
Encounters Network • Prayer Storm • Compassion Acts

PART ONE

ARMED FOR TODAY'S ADVENTURES IN THE PROPHETIC

Prophetic gifts are a necessary part of the equipment supplied by God so that we can participate in bringing His Kingdom to earth. Inevitably, our role in helping to establish the Kingdom involves spiritual warfare, because, "We know that we are of God, and that the whole world lies in the power of the evil one" (1 John 5:19 NASB). Armed with God's prophetic gifts, we will be equipped for victorious warfare under the direction of His Holy Spirit.

However, before we start wielding our prophetic swords, we need to root ourselves in the truths of God that are foundational to our life in the Spirit. With the burning passion of true Gospel messengers to communicate the basics of life-giving truth, the authors of the following chapters will both review what you already know and expand your horizons.

Each of us (even those of us who do not feel particularly adventuresome) needs to know how to lay hold of a variety of gifts from God's storehouse. The chapters you are about to read will take you down the hallway and give you a chance to peek behind some new doorways and thus encourage you in your personal quest for spiritual success in this great venture.

Chapter 1

POWER OF THE PROPHETIC
James W. Goll

I was one of the speakers at a signs and wonders conference in Bangkok, Thailand. The daytime meetings were in an Anglican Church and the evening renewal meetings were at a large YMCA.

With the help of an interpreter, I was in the middle of my presentation at one of the first evening meetings when my attention was drawn—it felt like a magnetic field—to a particular woman over in the corner. I kept trying to preach, but I couldn't get away from the annoying feeling that I needed to stop in the middle of my talk and pay attention to her. From previous experience, I have learned to yield to the leading of the Holy Spirit when that happens. Thinking, *I'm a few thousand miles from home, so what difference does it make anyway?* I decided to take the risk of looking foolish. So I stepped away from the podium, walked toward her, took her by the hand, and pulled her to her feet.

I started prophesying over her, pronouncing a "Mother Teresa anointing" upon her and declaring that she was going to be used to go to the trash heaps of life to find treasures for Jesus, that she would rescue young girls who had been sold by their parents for money into the sex trade, that she would set them free from darkness, and that she would be involved in helping to break up sex slave operations in Thailand. At that time, I did not really know much about the magnitude of Thailand's sex slave business.

I was prophesying so fast that it seemed as if my interpreter must have been using both the gifts of translation and interpretation. As he translated, people all around the room began to weep and laugh all at the same time. I did not have a clue of what was actually transpiring, but it was apparent that something good was taking place!

Confirmation of the word was almost immediate. The next day Wesley Campbell (who was one of the other speakers) and I actually got to go visit a "house of rescue" that this lady had started. The police were bringing her young girls who had been raised in the sex slave environment. As a result of living in the house of rescue, the girls were getting saved, filled with the Holy Spirit, healed, and delivered. They were the treasures I had prophesied about!

We interviewed some of these beautiful young girls who had been ravaged by who knows how many men. Through translators, we asked them, "What do you want to do when you grow up?"

Every single one of them answered the same way: "Oh, I want to have a house that saves girls from the sex slavery business." One of the things I had prophesied over the founder was that she would have a whole lineage of houses that were sort of like orphanages. What confirmation! Needless to say, the entire prophecy had brought much edification, joy, courage, and affirmation to that dear woman, showing her that God wanted her to keep on doing what she was doing. In Jesus' eyes, she was giving such a great testimony about Him that He had decided to give a testimony about her, so He used the power of the prophetic gift to do so.

Day Two

The next day, the whole atmosphere of the place was charged with expectation. These people had watched the other prophecy and now they thought I could call anybody out by name, birth date, and Social Security number. I did not want to disappoint them, but I was going to need all the help God could give me, because I didn't have much to go on.

In fact, only one thing kept cycling around in my mind. Finally I spoke it out: "There is a seventeen-year-old boy, a son of someone here, and he is backslidden and on drugs. He is going to give himself to the Lord tonight."

Nothing happened. Everybody was looking at me but nobody was responding. I'm sure they were wondering why that one didn't work like the one the night before. I waited a minute and then I decided it would be safer to go back to preaching, so I did.

The trouble is, I didn't get much farther before that same word started circling around inside of me again—seventeen-year-old boy, backslidden, on drugs, son of someone here, et cetera. So I stopped preaching again and, with the help of my interpreter, I released the word once more. No one responded, not even a mother.

So, I commenced praying in tongues quietly as I went back to preaching, briefly. I was beginning to think that what had happened earlier had messed up the expectations of the group, and now people were expecting me to be able to pull any bunny out of any hat. Then that word started circulating inside me again.

That convinced me that this must really be a word from God, because that is how it works. So I launched out a third time. Once again, I ended up looking like a fool. Inside, I was thinking, *This is a true word. So would somebody please quit denying the truth and 'fess up?* All I could do was complete my message. We sang a few more worship songs and the meeting was finished for the evening.

After the close of the meeting, I was supposed to leave the auditorium and go back to my hotel to bed because I had to teach again the next day. But somehow I could not leave. That same word was *still* cycling around and around in my tired head. Finally, almost everybody had left. A young janitor came into the auditorium to put the chairs away. I got into a conversation with him, because he spoke English.

Turns out he was seventeen years old. And he was on drugs. And he was a backslider. And he had actually rededicated his life to Jesus that night. He had been there, hanging around the back of the auditorium and listening to the meeting, and he had realized that word was for him. He just didn't say so in public.

Jesus is a great fisherman. It did not matter that the prophetic preacher did not look like he knew what he was doing. Just the day before I had looked like Superman, and now I looked like Clark Kent. But it did not matter because the pure power of the prophetic word had testified of Jesus' power again. My reputation was beside the point. When you take risks and prophesy, you will gain and lose your reputation a hundred times over. The most important thing is that the testimony of Jesus gets released and that God gets worshiped in the process.

PURPOSE OF PROPHETIC POWER

We can find this stated in Scripture in so many words:

> …*For the testimony of Jesus is the spirit of prophecy* (Revelation 19:10).

I quote this line often—and also to the lines that come before it in that chapter of the Book of Revelation. Earlier in the text, we find ourselves before God's throne in Heaven, worshiping with the heavenly host:

> *And the twenty-four elders and the four living creatures fell down and worshiped God who sat on the throne, saying, "Amen! Alleluia!" Then a voice came from the throne, saying, "Praise our God, all you His servants and those who fear Him, both small and great!"*
>
> *And I heard, as it were, the voice of a great multitude, as the sound of many waters and as the sound of mighty thunderings, saying, "Alleluia! For the Lord God Omnipotent reigns!*

Let us be glad and rejoice and give Him glory, for the marriage of the Lamb has come, and His wife has made herself ready." And to her it was granted to be arrayed in fine linen, clean and bright, for the fine linen is the righteous acts of the saints.

Then he said to me, "Write: 'Blessed are those who are called to the marriage supper of the Lamb!'" (Revelation 19:4-9)

In an atmosphere of the highest worship, we hear that the Bride (the Church) has made herself ready for her marriage to the Lamb (Jesus). She has embraced the free gift of righteousness through the blood of the Lamb, and she has also furthered her preparation through her righteous acts, walking out the reality of the righteousness that He has won for her.

Moving on, we read that line about the testimony of Jesus being the spirit of prophecy, but before that we have also found out that the pure purpose of the prophetic is *to help the Bride make herself ready.* Jesus is coming for an equally yoked Bride, one who has clothed herself with "fine linen, clean and bright," which is her righteous acts. She needs both the gift (something she did not earn) and the acts (something she chooses to do).

This is not salvation by works; rather this is works matching faith and faith being demonstrated by acts of righteousness. The Bride/Church is going to be invited to the marriage supper of the Lamb because she has made herself ready. In essence, the purpose of the prophetic is *to bring the Bride into intimacy with God.*

Now the apostle John, who was writing all of these revelations down, says he was overcome with the spirit of worship at this point. He fell down at the feet of the angel who had been speaking, only to be told, "See that you do not do that! I am your fellow servant, and of your brethren who have the testimony of Jesus. Worship God! *For the testimony of Jesus is the spirit of prophecy*" (Rev. 19:10). Do you see how that line appears in the context of the Bride making herself ready in both gifts and acts, faith and works? The worship, directed to God Himself and not to His messenger, is both the context and the response. —

JESUS WILL BE GLORIFIED

Worship creates the supernatural culture in which the voice of the Lord can be heard. Worship and intimacy with God have an enormous amount to do with the prophetic release. In fact, you can always tell if the true prophetic is flowing because it results in people giving testimony about how great Jesus is.

Another way of approaching the idea that the testimony of Jesus is the spirit of prophecy is to say that Jesus in essence raises His hand (just like one of us might do) when He wants to give a testimony. He raises His hand through one of us, through the exercise of the gift of prophecy. He lives inside us believers; we are new creations in Him. Jesus Christ is in you, the hope of glory (see Col. 1:27). After getting our attention, He testifies through our hearts, which overflow with His testimony so that we speak it out.

In summary, *the purpose of the prophetic is to release a testimony that glorifies Jesus.* Jesus, who is the same yesterday, today, and forever, testifies about Himself through the spirit of prophecy in one of His servants. By means of that testimony, He is glorified. The person who speaks that testimony declares how real and relevant and good He is. The gift of prophecy declares how good God is!

Whether the prophetic voice is expressed through public declarations, as I did in Thailand, or private encounters (through dreams, visions, angelic encounters, or fleeting senses), it all comes down to the same thing—Jesus' testifying to and through His servants.

People often explain the prophetic overflow as His word "bubbling up" on the inside, which is fitting since His word always flows from that living river that we all have inside. *"He who believes in Me, as the Scripture has said, out of his heart will flow rivers of living water"* (John 7:38).

Know Him and Make Him Known

When people who are unfamiliar with the prophetic movement hear the word "prophecy," they may think that it applies only to predicting the future. This is far from the only focus of prophecy, although it may be included as part of the revelatory package.

The pure and most powerful purpose of prophecy is to tell about a Man. It is to have a personal revelation of Jesus Christ and to carry a testimony about Him. It is to magnify the Son of God and get other things dropped in along the way, such as prediction of the future or impartation of power.

You see, when you are in an atmosphere of worship, you can see things that cannot be seen outside that dimension. You hear things that you might not hear under normal circumstances. You feel things that you might typically ignore. You look through life with a different lens. You are in a supernatural dimension!

Prophecy answers the question, "Who do people say that I am?" which is what Jesus asked Peter in Caesarea Philippi (see Matt. 16:13). On their own, people have various opinions about that question. The disciples reported some of them: "Some say John the Baptist, some Elijah, and others Jeremiah or one of the prophets" (Matt. 16:14). Most likely, they answered this way because they knew people who had seen in Jesus some of the attributes of John the Baptist, Elijah, and Jeremiah such as crying out in the wilderness, working miracles, or weeping and prophesying judgment.

But when Jesus asked, "But who do you say that I am?", it was time for Peter's prophetic reply (see Matt. 16:15).

> ..."You are the Christ, the Son of the living God." Jesus answered and said to him, "Blessed are you, Simon Bar-Jonah, for flesh and blood has not revealed this to you, but My Father who is in Heaven" (Matthew 16:16-17).

Clearly, Peter could not have known this on his own. His flesh and blood could not have figured it out. To help him answer the question, the Father had sent the Spirit to him with a "cheat sheet." Peter's heart had turned warm. He had spoken up with the revelation he had just received from Heaven, "You are the Christ, the Son of the living God." He himself did not entirely comprehend the statement, but as soon as he uttered it Jesus' response was, "Peter, you are blessed."

This was a personal, almost private moment. Prophetic words are like that. God reaches down personally and hands a person a cheat sheet. Holy Spirit to human spirit, He shows a person what he or she needs to know and He helps the person express it in words.

Later in the New Testament, Paul wrote, *"...no one can say that Jesus is Lord except by the Holy Spirit"* (1 Cor. 12:3). Good news! Simon Peter would not be the only person who could ever receive the revelation that Jesus is the Christ. The first person of the Godhead that we are allowed to meet is His Holy Spirit—so that every one of us can receive the revelation that Jesus Christ is Lord. The Spirit's job is to make Jesus real so that we can respond to Him personally. In other words, it takes God to know God.

PIERCING DEFENSES

God wants to use prophetic means to make Jesus real in the lives of men and women. One of the best examples of this happened as disciples were beginning to gather around Jesus. Andrew and his brother Simon Peter had found Him first. Then the next day Philip, who came from the same city, Bethsaida, found Him. Eager to share the news, Philip went and found Nathanael and told him:

> ... *"We have found Him of whom Moses in the law, and also the prophets, wrote—Jesus of Nazareth, the son of Joseph." And Nathanael said to him, "Can anything good come out of Nazareth?" Philip said to him, "Come and see." Jesus saw Nathanael coming toward Him, and said of him, "Behold,*

an Israelite indeed, in whom is no deceit!" Nathanael said to Him, "How do You know me?" Jesus answered and said to him, "Before Philip called you, when you were under the fig tree, I saw you." Nathanael answered and said to Him, "Rabbi, You are the Son of God! You are the King of Israel!" Jesus answered and said to him, "Because I said to you, 'I saw you under the fig tree,' do you believe? You will see greater things than these." And He said to him, "Most assuredly, I say to you, hereafter you shall see Heaven open, and the angels of God ascending and descending upon the Son of Man" (John 1:45-51).

Whereas the first three men were convinced instantly (...this Jesus really could be the long-awaited Messiah!), Nathanael was skeptical—until Jesus' prophetic words pierced his defenses.

Nathanael must have been disappointed earlier in his life, because he had his defenses up. If he had lived in Tennessee where I do, his twenty-first-century reaction might have been, "Come on, you guys, give me a break! Are you trying to tell me that this ordinary rabbi is the same Messiah that Moses and the prophets talked about? All kinds of people have claimed to be the Messiah. Anyway, can anything good come out of Murfreesboro?"

Jesus brushed his skepticism aside by saying, essentially, "Hey there, I like your heart. It's not the least bit deceitful. And by the way, I saw you under the fig tree."

This startled Nathanael. His reaction was, "How do You know me? How did you get my mail?" This is just the reaction that the prophetic is supposed to produce.

Jesus' gaze had penetrated Nathanael's heart. Even though Nathanael was inclined to reject Him, Jesus appreciated the fact that he was not a fake. Nathanael was not a religious farce. He said what he meant and he did not play games. He told the truth as he saw it. So even though Nathanael's first reaction was disbelief, Jesus penetrated his defenses with a simple word of knowledge about him sitting under a fig tree.

Jesus, the perfect prophet, did this same kind of thing with the woman he met at the well in Samaria (see John 4:1-26). She really did not want to talk with Him, and she had many reasons. But Jesus broke down her resistance gradually. His comments about living water did not make much sense to her, and she could have just picked up her water container and left the scene. But then Jesus set her up for a word of knowledge:

> *Jesus said to her, "Go, call your husband, and come here." The woman answered and said, "I have no husband." Jesus said to her, "You have well said, 'I have no husband,' for you have had five husbands, and the one whom you now have is not your husband; in that you spoke truly." The woman said to Him, "Sir, I perceive that You are a prophet"* (John 4:16-19).

With that, suddenly she was willing to listen to anything He had to say, and she went to summon the rest of the townspeople to hear Him as well.

> *And many of the Samaritans of that city believed in Him because of the word of the woman who testified, "He told me all that I ever did."…the Samaritans…urged Him to stay with them; and He stayed there two days. And many more believed because of His own word"* (John 4:39-41).

True prophetic revelation broke down defenses and made it possible for the woman and townspeople to respond to Jesus' message, acknowledging Him not only as a prophet but also as the Messiah. Revelatory giftings are like anti-tank missiles, coming in to shatter the enemy's schemes and expose darkness, releasing freedom to captives.

A Place at the Table

Jesus' revelatory words were very simple. He told Nathanael that he was an honest man who had just been sitting under a fig tree. He told the Samaritan woman that she had lived with many men. Our prophetic words can be simple, too.

We do not have to find "deep" vocabulary or go into great detail (although it can happen on occasion). Like my friend Patricia King (you can read about this in Chapter 5), your most powerful prophetic word may be as simple as "God loves you with an everlasting love." The impact of a prophetic word does not come from eloquence or loudness or even from how many people hear it. The power comes from the fact that the word originates with God and that its results glorify God. True words from God are very personal, highly encouraging, and often quite simple.

Each of us has a special place in God's Kingdom, and He directs His attention to us in turn. That reminds me of something He showed me not long ago.

My father owned a lumberyard, and even though he did not have much money he and my mother were able to build a new house for our family in 1959. I was seven years old when we moved into our new place. In the fifties, one of the popular colors was turquoise, and this new house was turquoise. So was our 1956 Ford. So was a lot of our furniture. Our whole kitchen was turquoise, too.

Our family life was not the greatest, but we did eat supper together around the kitchen table (in the turquoise kitchen). Each family member had a place. Daddy was at one end. Momma sat right around the corner at his left hand because she could easily get up from there to go fetch whatever we needed. My one sister sat next to my mom and my little sister sat next to me. I sat at my father's right hand. I didn't think about the significance of that at the time. Now I find it amazingly symbolic that my place as the only son was to sit at my earthly father's right hand.

You see, in the Father's house, each of us has a special place to sit. Your place is just for you, not for anyone else. It has a nametag on it. I am not thinking only of your place in Heaven, although you have a place there, too. I am talking about your place in the family of God here on earth. Just as your place is for you, so is your purpose. The words you will hear from God have been directed to you alone, and they are distinctive.

Once I had a dream about sitting around that kitchen table in the turquoise Goll kitchen. In the dream, I heard a song being played, "Hallelujah, for the Lord God Almighty Reigns," and I heard my mom across the table (who loved to sing) singing along. Then in my dream, I heard another voice entering in with her. It was my dad, who in real life did not meet Jesus until later in life, singing along with her. It was an amazing duet for sure.

Then as the dream continued, all of a sudden at the other end of the table, Michael W. Smith materialized, and he joined in with my parents. Now they were singing his song, "Agnus Dei," and it had become a trio. I woke up knowing not only that some songs are written in Heaven and transcribed by humble servants such as Michael W. Smith (who happens to be one of my dear personal friends), but also that although there was a lot of discord in our family on earth, my mom and dad are in unity now singing a duet in Heaven before the One who saved them by His great grace.

God has designated a special seat at His table for you, and with His personal touch He will communicate His love to you there. His Spirit will keep on coming to meet you as long as you keep coming to meet Him.

PROPHETIC POWER GETS RESULTS

Prophecy can take all kinds of forms, and it is not the purpose of this book to define them like a textbook. But the purpose of prophecy—to edify, comfort, exhort, and to release a testimony of Jesus—runs through every true word from God. Every true word from God carries power and gets results. The challenge is telling the true from the false—or simply pointless—words.

Do you want to know how to receive prophetic words that get results? One way to identify the powerful ones is that they are like flypaper. In other words, you can't get them off you. Or, rather, you *can* get them off you, but only by putting them on someone else. And then another piece of flypaper comes and sticks to you, and so on. You can have a lot of adventures with prophetic flypaper! The testimony of Jesus is like flypaper.

For example, right after communism lifted I went to Albania and spent several weeks teaching leaders in several cities about the present-day ministry of the Holy Spirit. In one city built on a cliff overlooking the Adriatic Sea, Shëngjin (Albanian for St. John), tradition held that Paul, Titus, and also John the Beloved had preached there. I was going to be part of the first public meeting of recent history where the gospel of the Kingdom of Jesus Christ would be proclaimed.

In the cold February rain, we climbed what was almost like a cliff to get to the community building that was the meeting place. The building had big, thick old walls. It was so cold in there that everyone in the audience had kept their winter coats on.

I had been praying for some word from Jesus for these people who had gone for so long without one. As I entered the building, the name "Sarah" went through my mind. I had expected something for the whole city or at least for the whole group of people who were coming to hear us. But all I got was "Sarah," again flowing through my mind.

At the entrance, we passed a female security guard who was chain-smoking. She was a massive, muscular woman, built like an Olympic shot-putter on steroids. Inside, we found out that we had no worship team, no source of worship music. There I was in this city where they had not heard the open proclamation of the gospel of Jesus Christ for scores of years. I got up, cold turkey, to preach. I looked out on the people, all of whom had dark hair and dark eyes and who were wearing their hats and coats. I thought I would talk about God's remedy for rejection, because they had been such an oppressed people.

But before I got very far in my message with my young interpreter at my side, the name "Sarah" went through my mind again. I said to him, "How do you pronounce the name Sarah in the Albanian language?" He said, "Oh, it is Sabrina."

So I stopped preaching and with the help of the interpreter, I asked, "Is anyone here named Sabrina?" Thank God, a lady three-fourths of the way back in the middle raised her hand. I did not have anything beyond her name, so I said, "Sabrina, stand up!" She stood up. I still didn't have anything. So I said, "Sabrina, step out into the aisle." After it was interpreted, Sabrina stepped out into the aisle. I still didn't have anything more for her, though, so I said, "Sabrina, come forward."

Everyone knew who Sabrina was. She had beautiful dark hair and dark eyes and she came forward wearing her thick winter coat. As she stood in front of me, I spoke privately to my interpreter again, saying, "I know a man should never ask a woman how old she is. How old do you think she is?"

He said, "You must understand that in Albania, the people have been oppressed for so long that they look older than they actually are. I would guess that she's 28."

I told him what to translate for her: "Your name is Sabrina. You have never heard the gospel of the Lord Jesus Christ ever in your life. You are thirty-two years old. You have a tumor in your left breast and Jesus wants to heal you."

Sabrina had never been in a Christian meeting, especially not in a charismatic-type meeting. Without ever having seen it anyplace before, she started shaking under the power of God. Every word was true: her name, her age, her medical condition, and the fact that she had never before heard the gospel message. The other people in the room knew it was true because they knew Sabrina. The power of the Holy Spirit came upon her and she gave her heart to Jesus in front of everybody that night.

I never got back to my preaching. The Spirit fell on two elderly gypsy women in the front row, and they came up to me and repented and gave their hearts to Jesus. Pretty soon everybody in the whole place was running toward me, all wanting God's touch. Did they all get saved? I don't know. Many did, and everyone there that night had a real experience with the real Jesus through the power of the prophetic gift.

After the meeting was over, the female security guard escorted me and my interpreter friend back down the hill. She successfully maneuvered us down the rain-drenched hill to the street below and left us by the curb. Our next goal was to find a taxi late at night to get from this city to the next city, where we were lodging. How were we going to find a taxi? It was raining and very dark because there were no streetlights. So we prayed and stuck out our thumbs.

A guy pulled over for us. We got in and the thought crossed my mind, *This is like in the Book of Acts when Philip got into that chariot and read that guy's mail. Here I am, getting into the chariot....*

I sat in the front seat and my interpreter friend sat in the back and we set off driving in the rain, trying to avoid the potholes. Through the interpreter, I started to tell the driver about what had just happened, about how a woman had come to a meeting and she had met a man named Jesus whom she had never heard about (it had turned out that she was a Muslim) and she had come to faith in Him. I told Him that Jesus knew how old she was and that she had a tumor in her breast and that He wanted to heal her. Then I said, "And her name was Sabrina."

Now this man started trembling and shaking under the power of the Holy Spirit. The taxi driver was Sabrina's husband! I got to lead Sabrina's husband to Jesus while he drove the car in the rain. That was another prophetic appointment if I ever had one!

Come, Holy Spirit

When you are walking in the will of God, this sort of divine appointment happens all the time, although in a variety of ways.

Before my wife went home to be with the Lord, she and I often traveled together to speak at conferences. Once we had an important conference looming on the horizon. It was in another state and Michal Ann had been given equal billing with me as a speaker. So she kept asking the Lord what He wanted her to speak about to the people.

She just couldn't discern what He wanted her to say. Time was growing short, and she needed to know. Her free time was such a precious resource, with our four children all still at home and me so often leaving on trips, plus she was overseeing our ministry finances. She knew, of course, that the busy-ness of her life would not suffice as an excuse when the time of the conference came.

She hoped that maybe the Lord would speak to her in her dreams, because often that was the best time for her to hear Him. Nothing. This dragged on for more than a month. Just two weeks before the conference, she had a dream in which she heard me asking a classroom full of people, "How do you hear the voice of the Holy Spirit?" In the dream, her heart leaped inside and she raised her hand and said, "I know! Let me tell them! I know how to hear the Holy Spirit." In the dream, I was in the middle of leaving the room for some reason, so I said to her, "Michal Ann, go ahead and tell the people how to hear the voice of the Holy Spirit. You can answer that question."

She awoke from the dream with a feeling of electric energy flowing over her body, and she recognized that feeling because it had happened before when God had dispatched angels to give her messages in the night. She knew that God had put a deposit inside her. She also remembered an old song based on a line from the New Testament:

Whatsoever things are true, whatsoever things are honest, whatsoever things are just, whatsoever things are pure, whatsoever things are lovely, whatsoever things are of good report; if there be any virtue, and if there be any praise, think on these things (Philippians 4:8 KJV).

Then she thought about the purpose of a tuning fork and realized that the Lord has planted a tuning fork inside each one of us as a fixed measure and starting point for our days. As in a symphony, each of us joined together with the rest of the spiritual body, and we are tuned to the same tuning fork so that we will be calibrated to the same true pitch—and the "tuning fork" can be found in Philippians 4:8. As each of us calibrates our lives to whatever is true, honest, just, pure, lovely, of good report, virtuous, and praiseworthy, we are tuning our hearts to hear God's voice and to join with others in transmitting it. That is what she talked about at the conference. God had revealed it to her prophetically, and it was about how to hear Him prophetically.

In Him we live and move and have our beings (see Acts 17:28). Jesus is raising His hand right now to testify to that truth by saying this: "In *you* I live and breathe and move and have My being."

It Takes God to Know God

You are a candidate for a prophetic life because it takes God to know God and you have His Spirit living inside you. Breathe Him in and then breathe out His word of truth. Listen to His word through your brothers and sisters. Join me, Mickey Robinson, Patricia King, Jeff Jansen, Ryan Wyatt, and others and become part of the greatest ride of your life—with us, venture into the prophetic!

Chapter 2

PERILS OF THE PROPHETIC

James W. Goll

Can we ever get it right?

I was ministering in a meeting one time, and by the end I thought I had laid hands on every single person, making sure to bless everybody. But I had skipped one person by mistake. The rest of the people went home rejoicing, but this one felt left out. More than that, he felt so thoroughly rejected that he ended up harboring a grudge against me for years. Eventually, he approached me in another meeting and repented to me and I forgave him. Until then, though, I hadn't known about the problem.

What did this teach me? Never to skip someone again? How could I guarantee that? Mistakes are a given. No doubt I will continue to stumble as I minister prophetically, just as I stumble in other ways. No human being is perfect, even the giants of the faith I admire so much.

From that experience and many others, I learned that we need simply to give each other a lot of grace. It has helped me to have experienced both sides of ministry myself. For instance, I had probably prophesied over a few thousand people before anyone ever prophesied over me in a public meeting, and then God used an anonymous woman to do it. It was not a great word, either, and I did not even get to hear the whole word because I fell down without a catcher.

Many of you, whether or not you have ever ministered prophetically in public, have had the same kind of humbling experience. You always make sure to get into the healing line, but you never get any attention. The rest of the people are lying there, resting in the Spirit, some of them having wonderful encounters with God, and there you are, still standing and looking around, wondering what to do next. It can become a pattern, but it is only a test. Will you trust God anyway? Will you keep coming to Him, or will you give up? Will you resist the temptation to derive your confidence from your prophetic experiences only?

REALITY CHECK

Prophetic experiences are fun, awe-inspiring, and amazing. They pierce defenses and open up avenues of faith, shifting the atmosphere and creating a culture of supernatural life. Prophetic words edify, build up, comfort, and give guidance. Yet sometimes afterward you wonder, "Where did You go, God?" because you cannot find Him anymore. Worse than that, you can find yourself facing serious hostility. How can something so wonderful open the door to so much trouble?

An obscure passage is buried in the Book of Hosea:

> *Let Israel know this! The prophet is a fool, the inspired man is demented, because of the grossness of your iniquity, and because your hostility is so great. Ephraim was a watchman with my God, a prophet; yet the snare of a bird catcher is in all his ways, and there is only hostility in the house of his God* (Hosea 9:7-8 NASB).

That is not exactly what you were looking for, is it? Not many of us will post that one on the refrigerator! Why do "snares" and "hostility" follow a prophet?

One reason is fairly obvious: because the prophet speaks the word of the Lord and people do not want to hear it. People are sinful. The original sin of humankind stands in rebellion against God's word. Hostility seethes in the sinful human heart against the intrusive entrance of God's word, because God's word speaks about "change" and change is a fearful prospect. Such words are often directive, or at least invitational, and when they elicit a negative reaction from their hearers, the prophet-messenger gets the blame.

One time I was in Guatemala and I was suffering from an attack of vertigo. Every morning I would wake up to a room that was swirling. I knew it was a physical problem, but I asked God for a spiritual connection and He spoke to me. He said, "I have not called you to balance the Church. I have called you to change the equilibrium of the Church."

Anytime you become one who announces new things or an agent of change, you can expect people to get upset. People do not like to have their equilibrium altered, even when it is their all-loving God who is doing it.

So That No One May Boast

Another reason that hostility follows a prophetic word is because of the offensive way the word may be packaged.

Moses was a Hebrew, but he grew up as an Egyptian prince in Pharaoh's house. So when he began to make requests on behalf of the slave population ("Let My people go!"), it was offensive to Pharaoh. Like Peter and Paul later, Moses was Jewish to the core, but God tapped each of those good Jews to reach into the Gentile world (see Gal. 2:7-8). It is amazing how often this happens, regardless of what teachers will say in seminary classes on cross-cultural missiology. ("Go to the people you are the most like. You are the best one to build bridges with those people. Keep it as homogeneous as possible….")

God just seems to like to mix it up. When He is not sending Jews to reach Gentiles, He is sending the educated to reach the uneducated—and the uneducated to reach those who have a lot of education. Paul wrote to the Corinthians:

*Think of what you were when you were called. Not many of
you were wise by human standards; not many were influen-
tial; not many were of noble birth. But God chose the foolish
things of the world to shame the wise; God chose the weak
things of the world to shame the strong. He chose the lowly
things of this world and the despised things—and the things
that are not—to nullify the things that are, so that no one
may boast before Him* (1 Corinthians 1:26-29 NIV).

This passage makes a statement about you and me. We are the foolish
ones, the lowly and despised and weak ones. The good part is that your
very weaknesses are what qualify you to be used by God. John Wimber
used to say, "I am a fool for Christ. Whose fool are you?" Whenever you
step out in faith, you will appear to be foolish to somebody. So just accept
it and rejoice in your humility.

God uses strange means to get His word across sometimes. After all, He
is God, and His ways are not our ways, nor are His thoughts our thoughts
(see Isa. 55:8). He does not like to be boxed in. (I like to say that He lived
in a box only once, in the Ark of the Covenant, and once He got out, He
vowed never to live in a human-made box again.) But He has chosen to live
in human hearts, and that means that when He presents His word, which
is already radical and different, He uses messengers who can come across
in strange and unusual ways.

I am putting myself in that category for sure. My wife used to tell me
that I had the ministry of sanity because I made other people feel sane. I
theorize that maybe God got bored, so He made prophets.

Besides, God speaks in such veiled ways that it almost seems to guarantee that people will stumble. He says, *"Hear now My words: if there is a
prophet among you, I, the Lord, make Myself known to him in a vision; I
speak to him in a dream"* (Num. 12:6). You know what? Dreams and visions
are hard to understand. Even when you think you understand one, usually
you do not get the whole meaning. The only logical response is to humbly

seek God's face. Speaking through dreams and visions turns out to be a perfect way for Him to create the grace of humility and seeking hearts.

When our children were little, my wife experienced nine weeks straight of angelic visitations every night. At the end, she received a promise from God. He said, "I will visit you again, but the next time I will come Myself." That sounded glorious, and we looked for another season of visitation, but it didn't happen the way we expected. Yet God is true to His word. He came Himself in September of 2008 and He took her home! I do not understand it and I have a million questions. But I am going to let those questions drive me to Him instead of away from Him.

These kinds of inconsistencies and surprises create the grace of humility, which is the opposite of hostility. We get to choose between humility or hostility as we respond to prophetic experiences.

THE PROPHETIC STRUGGLE

The perennial prophetic predicament involves negative reactions on the parts of both the hearers of a prophetic word and the prophets themselves. Snares and hostilities abound because of a lack of appreciation for how the prophetic process works and how many things can go awry with it.

Problems can arise at any of the three progressive stages of a prophetic word: revelation, interpretation, or application. The risk to the prophet seldom occurs because of inappropriate self-promotion or aggrandizement. Rather, the risk comes from the negative responses of others—and the corresponding reactions from the person who delivered the prophetic word.

A prophetic person is always just a human being, as are his or her critics. So the prophetic person can react to criticism in negative ways, such as becoming adversarial, deciding to operate outside the ranks of the Church, releasing judgmental words, or becoming isolated and insubordinate.

I seem to be in touch with hundreds of prophets like this. They are the ones with the unredemptive, doomsday words. Sadly, their words no longer reflect the heart of the Father. They shout, "The economy is shaking!" Yes, it is. But does it require a prophet to tell you that? Does it require a prophet to tell you, "There's a hole in the dike right now!"

When a prophet becomes adversarial, judgmental, critical, and isolated (outside the Church), people further refuse the words of that person. The reactions and counter-reactions go on, making the Church into a "non-prophet" organization more and more.

God's intention, however, is for the prophetic ministries, as well as the other ministries listed in Scripture, to operate in a team context with peers and friends within the Body of Christ who supply mutual support, humility in course-correction, reciprocal blessing, and the safety net of a caring community. He wants prophets to carry the wisdom of the sons of Issachar as they speak words that will help people follow God through times of trial (see 1 Chron. 12:32). This is far different from having hostile church people standing against prophets, who retreat in isolation and rejection.

Perhaps in these days, the equilibrium is changing. If nothing else, people from both sides are coming to better understand prophetic dynamics, and prophets are learning to couch their revelations less as ultimatums or harangues and more as words of wisdom, counsel, or godly suggestions.

Personal Snares

A good part of the prophetic struggle involves personal identity. People tend to identify themselves by what they do: "I am a prophet." Then when hostilities erupt, the prophet takes it personally. This can happen with any of the spiritual gifts.

To avoid the pitfalls inherent in deriving too much security from your identity as a prophet, you need to examine your foundation for your life in Christ. Who are you in Christ Jesus? Who is He in you? Your identity is not in what you *do*, it is in who you *are* in Him. You are not what you do. You are loved because of grace, not because of how well you perform or how dynamic your gifting may be. I have struggled personally with this one.

When you find your security and identity in Jesus, then when a task is finished you will not capitulate with an identity crisis because of a faulty foundation. When you are "in Christ," who is unshakable, you can stand firm in the face of fierce storms of disapproval. You won't feel the need to defend yourself. In fact, you will be able to ask God for wisdom with which to respond to your opponents. Everything that can be shaken will be shaken in order to shake out everything that is not founded on Jesus (see Heb. 12:27). But the Kingdom of God is unshakable.

The fact is that your function will change over time. You cannot say, "Once a pastor, always a pastor (or marketplace leader, or deacon, or whatever)." Philip was a deacon and he became an evangelist. Anybody who has accumulated very many years as a Christian has changed functions more than once. You must be a flexible new wineskin in God's hands, ready to have something new poured in. You must be able to expand even as you die daily.

When a prophetic person stakes too much of his or her identity on personal prophetic function the result can be stubbornness and dogmatism, not so much because the person is rebellious or wicked, but simply because the person is trying to survive. Eventually, an unteachable spirit can settle in. ("I hear from God and I learn from no man.") The person may start to add, "Thus saith the Lord!" or "God says," much more often and more loudly than before, with more emotion, or even with a little arrogance.

Too often, the problem is complicated by the idea that the only "real" prophetic ministry is a public one. With public ministry as the goal, perceived rejections pile up more quickly. In actuality, although all of us are called to full-time ministry within the context of our secular jobs and raising families, less than 1 percent of all Christians are called to full-time vocational ministry. If people consider the highest form of prophetic release to be a spontaneous, ecstatic word spoken on a public platform, they have narrowed the scope of prophetic ministry to almost zero.

All of us are called to function in faith at home, at work, at school—everywhere we go. In those contexts, the highest form of prophetic release may well be prophetic intercession. You pray your prophecy. You pray your vision. You change history before the throne of God. You also listen for your own life, and God makes Himself known to you. Instead of striving to become the best public speaker or the most accurate prophet, you will then desire most of all to make Jesus known to others. Secure in your identity as His beloved child, you can spend yourself spreading His love to others.

GOING TO THE SOURCE

From the point of view of both the giver and the receiver, the way to handle prophetic ministry is to go to the Source, the Lord Himself. This was the advice of the apostle John:

> *Beloved, do not believe every spirit, but test the spirits, whether they are of God; because many false prophets have gone out into the world. By this you know the Spirit of God: Every spirit that confesses that Jesus Christ has come in the flesh is of God, and every spirit that does not confess that Jesus Christ has come in the flesh is not of God* (1 John 4:1-3).

Practically speaking, what does this mean? Consider a revelation (and its presentation) and decide, not whether it suits your tastes or offends you, but rather:

- What is the heart of the issue? What ideas, concepts, teachings, or information came forth?

- What does the message release? What are the results of the message? What is its fruit?

- Is the Cross of Christ central? Is it presented as the source of new life?

- Can you discern God's love in the message?

- Does the message lead you to the Source, or does it lead you into distraction?

You do not have to hurry. No one is testing your response time. You have the Holy Spirit dwelling inside you, and He will help you. You do not have to imitate anybody else or rely on someone else to spoon-feed you with an acceptable response.

As a prophet yourself, remember that your prophetic gifting does not make you immune from mistakes. You need to be able to hear God correct you when necessary. Remember that, regardless of your prophetic prowess, you are like anyone else in relating one-to-one with God. Even if you are a highly-acclaimed prophet or apostle or the manager of intergalactic stratospheres, you live on the same plane as everyone else.

It's all about a relationship.

An opposite, equally important point is this: Do not become a prophecy junkie. The revelatory word complements the written Word of God. Become a Word-aholic and let the revelatory gifting be the icing on the cake rather than the main course.

Reviewing the Nature of the Prophetic

If you want to build a skyscraper, you have to make sure you first build a foundation that is strong, firm, and very deep. In the same way, if you want to reach the prophetic heights, you need to pay a lot of attention to the basics. Let's do a quick review of the nature of the prophetic:

1. Most words are invitations to respond to God with conditions that first must be met. Very few are declarations that something will happen automatically.

2. Very few words are immediate, "now" words. Most are words that help people in the process of change.

3. Few words get people out of their dilemmas. Instead, they shed light, give comfort and encouragement, and generally provide the light to carry on. There are no shortcuts with God.

4. Our focus should be not on the word of promise but on the God who promised. We need to direct our faith toward the God of the word. When our faith is misplaced, it produces unreal expectations.

5. Recognize that every promise contains a cost. This "clarity and cost equation" means that what God counts as most significant will often incur the greatest opposition by the enemy. Paul was warned repeatedly of how much he would suffer for Christ's sake.

6. Prophetic words are tokens or signposts that point the way to the One who is the Answer to every question. They are not meant to explain every jot or tittle of God's will.

7. True prophecy is partial (see 1 Cor. 13:9). True prophecy is also progressive. True prophecy has conditions that may remain unspoken.

8. Give room for "time lapse." As most words are invitations with an end in view, a built-in duration of time will need to elapse before the recipient has been prepared to receive the promise.

You can depend on the fact that true predictive words or words of promise will be fulfilled—maybe not in your lifetime, but eventually. I am keeping track of a lot of "pending" words. Most are also conditional. In other words, certain conditions need to be met before they can be fulfilled. In many cases, God will provide more than one chance for those conditions to be fulfilled, as He did with Jonah and Nineveh.

AVOIDING OVERREACTION

In any case, do not be too quick to throw out a prophetic word because you do not happen to like it, and do not throw out an entire word just because one element of it seems to be "off." Due to repeated errors and failures and abuses, the temptation can be to despise the whole mess, but hold off: *"Do not quench the Spirit. Do not despise prophecies"* (1 Thess. 5:19-20). Or, as the New International Version puts it: *"Do not put out the Spirit's fire; do not treat prophecies with contempt."* We must learn mature wisdom to avoid overreacting.

You see, in our response to prophetic words, we need to avoid two ditches on the sides of the road. One is the overreaction of becoming unsettled to the point of discarding or rejecting a word. The other is the overreaction of becoming enamored or captivated with it. Paul warned:

> *...We ask you, brothers, not to become easily unsettled or alarmed by some prophecy, report or letter supposed to have come from us, saying that the day of the Lord has already come* (2 Thessalonians 2:1-2 NIV).

Instead, "Test all things; hold fast what is good" (1 Thess. 5:21). Great benefit will come as we cultivate the character needed to carry the gift (see Eph. 4:1; 1 Tim. 2:2).

PARADOXES IN THE HALL OF FAME

To avoid prophetic perils and pitfalls, we need to remember that unseen, eternal things are more real than temporal ones that we can touch and see, and we take hold of the eternal things by faith. Our missteps and misunderstandings do not matter as much as our faith—which is another way of saying how tightly we hold onto the hand of God.

Some of the mightiest heroes of faith are listed in what is known as the "Faith Hall of Fame," the eleventh chapter of the letter to the Hebrews. The heroes listed here, some of whom go back almost to the beginning of humankind, are all prophetic people. Their lives present paradoxes to those of us who like everything to be black and white, neat and tidy, smooth and creamy. Near the end of the chapter, the descriptions get more violent:

> *And what more shall I say? For the time would fail me to tell of Gideon and Barak and Samson and Jephthah, also of David and Samuel and the prophets: who through faith subdued kingdoms, worked righteousness, obtained promises, stopped the mouths of lions, quenched the violence of fire, escaped the edge of the sword, out of weakness were made strong, became valiant in battle, turned to flight the armies of the aliens. Women received their dead raised to life again. Others were tortured, not accepting deliverance, that they might obtain a better resurrection. Still others had trial of mockings and scourgings, yes, and of chains and imprisonment. They were stoned, they were sawn in two, were tempted, were slain with the sword. They wandered about in sheepskins and goatskins, being destitute, afflicted, tormented—of whom the world was not worthy. They wandered in deserts and mountains, in dens and caves of the earth. And all these, having obtained a good testimony through faith, did not receive the promise, God having provided something better for us, that they should not be made perfect apart from us* (Hebrews 11:32-40).

These tormented souls present us with what seems like a contradiction. Reading about them, you wonder if the perils of the prophetic are just too numerous and too severe to be endured. And then you realize that these forerunners in the faith, even though they had not seen Jesus, kept going until the end, leaning into the truth they had obtained, leaning on the everlasting arms of the One who loved them so much that He put their stories in His written Word. Without knowing what it was, these mighty heroes of faith sensed the mysterious aroma of the Messiah who would come, whose Cross would become an eternal symbol of His redeeming love.

We who have come later in time have been blessed with a fuller measure of the Spirit. If they could do it, how much more can we? Sure, we may suffer some things. But we can keep leaning in to see what He has for us next. We can keep our eyes fixed on *"Jesus, the author and finisher of our faith,"* who will make sure that we do not stray (Heb. 12:2). *"For consider Him who has endured such hostility by sinners against Himself, so that you will not grow weary and lose heart"* (Heb. 12:3 NASB).

In fact, we can learn to "kiss the Cross," embracing the paradoxes and perils and risks of this adventure of faith. Go ahead, get a mouthful of splinters—kiss the Cross. Keep Jesus central. And always, always be ready to release that eternal fragrance of Christ (see 2 Cor. 2:15).

As prophetic people, our goal is not to be famous or to be the brightest and most accurate or best or highest. Our goal is that Jesus Christ may be made known. With a proper foundation, prophetic ministry can pour forth unimpeded until the Perfect One comes again! (See 1 Corinthians 13:10.)

Chapter 3

ENCOURAGEMENT: IMPARTING SPIRITUAL BRAVERY

Mickey Robinson

I am known best for my failed death.

I was in an airplane crash more than 40 years ago, and I survived with horrible injuries: serious burns, paralysis, brain damage, blindness, and many secondary problems. They gave me up to die.

I wasn't a Christian until I had an NDE—near-death supernatural experience. I was just a 19-year-old American heathen who was getting it on, trying to be Mr. Cool Skydiver until I got burned severely and developed multiple deadly complications. After exhausting all medical means to save me, they maintained me until I expired. I was thrust into a spiritual realm, seeing and feeling things I had no grid for, including absolute darkness and eternal separation from the Source of all life. On the edge of eternity I screamed out the same pathetic prayer I prayed in the ambulance: "I'm sorry; give me another chance." I stood in the Glory and Presence transformed by unfathomable love and power. God got my attention the hard way, but He really got it. (You can read the whole story in my book, *Falling to Heaven*.) Eventually, through a series of miracles and supernatural healings, I began to live a new-creation life.

When I was still in intensive care, one of my skydiver friends came to visit me. According to the rules only family members were allowed to come in, but he waited outside until they put him on a list so he could come in a few times. Each time he visited, he grabbed the only part of my body that was touchable and uninjured—my left hand—and he squeezed it. Every time he squeezed it, I felt power come into me. He did not say a word.

As it turned out, he would become a Spirit-filled Christian, and God's presence through him was ministering to me, which proves that the laying on of hands works anytime God's love is behind the gesture. There were no words he could have said anyway. He imparted encouragement and life to me as his love and God's love flowed into me.

EXHORTATION, ENCOURAGEMENT

Most of the time, God's messages of love and encouragement are conveyed through words that people speak or write to each other. By "encouragement," I mean a lot more than the sentiments on a greeting card. To encourage means to put courage into someone, and the origins of the word "courage" have to do with the word "heart." Encouragement puts heart into someone, and that includes life, love, and confidence.

Encouragement is one of the primary purposes of the gift of prophecy. It is one of the three pillars of prophecy: *edification* (which means up-building and strengthening), *encouragement* (also translated "exhortation"), and *comfort*. We find these in Paul's first letter to the Corinthians: *"He who prophesies speaks edification and exhortation and comfort to men"* (1 Cor. 14:3). Paul did not linger long on that definition. He was too busy giving encouragement to everyone he met, expressing words of edification, encouragement, and comfort every time he preached or conversed or wrote a letter.

The last thing that Paul wrote that got into the Bible is his second letter to his young protégé, Timothy. After greeting him with comforting words regarding his mother and grandmother, Paul wrote:

> *Therefore I remind you to stir up the gift of God which is in you through the laying on of my hands. For God has not*

given us a spirit of fear, but of power and of love and of a sound mind (2 Timothy 1:6-7).

Paul was exhorting Timothy to kindle afresh the spiritual gifts and graces that God had deposited in him.

Paul didn't know he was writing a book of the Bible. He was just expressing the heart of the Father to his son in the faith, Timothy. The whole letter is filled with encouragement. More than that, Paul was imparting spiritual bravery to Timothy. Writing from a dungeon in Rome, Paul knew that his life on earth was nearing its end. He talked about having run the race and finished the course. He had invested himself in Timothy, and he wanted him to carry on his work, working hard and bearing suffering for the sake of Christ.

Paul was not worried about his own fate; he was concerned that the work would continue. He viewed the work as telling people that God loves them, making sure they were walking in the grace of God, and continuing that until the end. To keep on doing the work of God and facing down numerous obstacles and discouragements, Paul knew that Timothy would need encouragement and sometimes extra courage.

All of us need spiritual bravery to live this life. We don't need hype. We don't need feel-good stuff. We definitely need more than "Christian Lite" advice, because:

> *We do not wrestle against flesh and blood, but against principalities, against powers, against the rulers of the darkness of this age, against spiritual hosts of wickedness in the heavenly places* (Ephesians 6:12).

We were born into unrelenting warfare and we need all the help we can get.

CALLED TO DO WHAT YOU CANNOT DO

God does not call you to do what you can do; He calls you to do what you *cannot* do apart from supernatural ability. Even if you have a lot of natural ability, He will call you to do something beyond your human strength.

That is because *He* wants to supply you with the requisite supernatural strength and boldness. He wants to replace your wavering human courage with true bravery. He intends to send much of His help through your brothers and sisters in Christ (some of whom have gone on before you, such as Paul).

You and your fellow believers can receive and give prophetic encouragement to each other as the Spirit supplies love and wisdom and words of life. *Prophetic encouragement* is just that: Spirit-supplied words that bubble up from the depths of your spirit and go out to satisfy the thirsty spirits and souls of the people around you, people whom God loves.

In order to accomplish this, you need to get into the flow of the river of God (see John 7:38). That river can refresh and sustain you to the point that your life will bubble up and overflow into the lives of others. When I was in Heaven, I saw the river of God. It was alive. It looked like it had golden radiation in it, and it was flowing right through me. I felt more alive then than I had ever felt before—more alive than being alive. I want that river of life to flow through me continuously here on earth, touching as many other people as possible wherever I go. I hope that you do, too.

SOUL AND SPIRIT

Your spirit is always looking for the headwaters of that river of life. The real you is a spirit. You have a soul and you live in a body of flesh. Your soul and your spirit are not the same thing. That's why the Bible tells us, *"the word of God is living and powerful, and sharper than any two-edged sword, piercing even to the division of soul and spirit..."* (Heb. 4:12). Your spirit is always tuning in for the right channel, the channel of Life. The right spiritual channel is the heavenly, eternal one.

Too many people settle for soulish things, sensual things of this earth, or religious pump-ups—things that will mean nothing in the long run. It seems to me that a lot of American Christianity is like Disneyland, with colorful banners and spotlights and entertainment and fun rides. You can ride all the rides and even visit exotic-seeming countries, but when it is time to go home you will find out that you have not really gone anywhere after all. You just had a lot of ups and downs.

However, when something gets imparted to you by the living word of God, it goes directly into your spirit. There is nothing hyped-up about it, and yet suddenly your spirit stands up and says, "Wait a minute! I am a new creature in Christ Jesus. I have been created for good works in Christ Jesus. I am walking on the road with God!" You have courage and perseverance and a sense of direction that will take you through the darkest night. Your spirit is both the transmitter and the receiver for prophetic encouragement.

Every human being has a spirit, not only the Christians. Therefore prophetic encouragement does not have to be directed toward Christians only—it can be for pre-Christians, too. In fact, I love to minister encouragement to the spirits of people who are not Christians. I look for opportunities. I fly on commercial airlines all the time and often I sit next to people who are a bit nervous about flying. When I tell them that I am a survivor of an airplane crash, they want to know anything I can tell them. Anybody who sees me knows that something terrible happened to me, so I have had this conversation many times.

Often I have been able to give prophetic encouragement to people on airplanes. They did not know what it was, of course. All they knew was that they benefited from talking with me and that what I told them helped them in some way. Sometimes I have led them to the Lord or have prayed for people to be healed or filled with the Holy Spirit.

So many people are boxed in with discouragement. Even Christians become dispirited, beaten down by circumstances and sometimes by preaching that tells them they are losers and they ought to feel guilty about it.

Prophetic encouragement works against discouragement the way light works against darkness. Whenever you introduce light, darkness just disappears. Let's say you have a brightly-lit room and into the middle of it you bring a box filled with darkness. When you open up the box, will the room get darker? Of course not. The light will shine into the box and illuminate it. Light is always superior to darkness.

God and light are synonymous (see 1 John 1:5). Through prophetic words, the brightness of the Spirit of God illuminates the darkness wherever the servants of God go. Thus the long-ago prophet Isaiah inscribed on his scroll:

> Arise, shine; for your light has come! And the glory of the Lord is risen upon you. For behold, the darkness shall cover the earth, and deep darkness the people; but the Lord will arise over you, and His glory will be seen upon you. The Gentiles shall come to your light, and kings to the brightness of your rising. "Lift up your eyes all around, and see: they all gather together, they come to you…" (Isaiah 60:1-4).

A word from God can penetrate even the hardest heart. If you don't believe it, just think about what happened to Saul (soon to be named Paul) on the road to Damascus. That guy was a true terrorist. He was hell-bent on destroying Christians. How long did it take God to melt his heart? Less time than it took you to read that sentence. With one flash of light from Heaven and a simple word, first from Jesus Himself and then through Ananias, Paul was a fanatic for Jesus. Don't worry about someone's heart being too hard; God knows how to plow!

FOR OTHERS' SAKES

People ask, "Why do I have to go to church?" Well, why do we? Why can't we simply pray and worship and be faithful Christians by ourselves at home?

The writer of the Book of Hebrews gives us an answer to that question. (We don't know who wrote that epistle, so the Holy Spirit can get total credit. It is a masterful bridge between the Old Testament and the New.) The reason for meeting with each other is simple:

> *Let us consider one another in order to stir up love and good works, not forsaking the assembling of ourselves together, as is the manner of some, but exhorting one another...* (Hebrews 10:24-25).

Other translations use the word "encouraging" in place of "exhorting."

In other words, when you meet with fellow believers, you put yourself in the best position to give and receive prophetic encouragement. Through each other, the Holy Spirit can minister life to the Body of Christ. The river of life can flow.

When we exhort and encourage each other with the up-building words that God's Spirit furnishes us, we impart courage to each other. We may have come together in a depleted condition, buffeted by the difficulties of life, but we leave ready for new challenges, closer to God, enabled to reach out with love.

When we assemble together, we do not do it just to make each other feel good or in order to "cope" better. Our goal is not to maintain the status quo. We want to be overcomers who equip each other to prevail over whatever we may be facing with fortitude and resolve. We want to see each other standing on top of our circumstances with shouts of victory.

I asked the Lord for a new definition of prophetic encouragement, and He showed me that *prophetic encouragement is the impartation of spiritual bravery.* It is! Spiritual bravery makes it possible for you to accept the assignments God gives you without fear. Called to do what you cannot do on your own strength, prophetic encouragement overrules your natural fearful reactions with the Spirit-inspired words and loving actions of your brothers and sisters in the faith.

Prophetic encouragement must become part of our lifestyle. Just as expressions of worship are not limited only to the people who have a natural sense of rhythm and musical ability, expressions of prophetic encouragement are not limited only to the natural optimists or "givers." Jesus said:

> *As the Father has loved Me, I have also loved you; abide in My love.... You are My friends if you do whatever I command you.... These things I command you, that you love one another* (John 15:9,14,17).

Anybody can express loving emotions, but when the Spirit of the Lord bubbles up in you and you impart to somebody an expression of His grace, causing him or her to light up and catch fire, suddenly becoming Braveheart material, you have done something that no human soul, no power of positive thinking, no motivational speaker can do. That's the power of prophetic encouragement, imparting spiritual bravery.

FIVE WORDS

Spiritual gifts have a variety of purposes. The gift of tongues, for example, enables you to pray according to the Spirit beyond your human capacity for comprehension. When you pray in tongues, you build up your own spirit in the power of the Holy Spirit. One way I know this is from personal experience.

I have a big lawn to mow, and I actually enjoy cutting the grass. I like the smell, and when I'm finished I always feel as though I have accomplished something because it looks nice. It is unlike most of the rest of what I work with, which is invisible and spiritual. A while back the muffler fell off my lawn mower, which made it really loud. I took advantage of it by praying in tongues as loudly as possible the whole time I was mowing. Nobody could hear me at all, but my kids laughed at me when they saw my mouth moving as I mowed back and forth, ducking under low tree branches and turning corners. I wonder why I felt extra good after mowing the lawn that time? I felt so good I almost went back and mowed it again.

I am very sure that Paul never mowed his lawn while he was speaking in tongues, but he said, "I thank God that I speak in tongues more than all of you" (1 Cor. 14:18 NIV). Immediately he added, "But in the church I would rather speak five intelligible words to instruct others than ten thousand words in a tongue" (1 Cor. 14:19 NIV).

In his view, a mere five words of prophetic instruction and encouragement were better than ten thousand words of equally inspired verbiage—because of the results. With a few well-placed words in a language the hearer can understand, holy energy and bravery can take root. A person can feel lower than a snake's basement looking for the crawl space underneath, but when they hear a true word of encouragement suddenly that person is standing on top of the roof declaring "Here I am! Send me!"

This can happen anytime that you let the river flow out of you into other people. The encouragement, empowered by the Spirit, builds and protects the other person's faith.

WHAT IF YOU ARE ALL ALONE?

It's all well and good to talk about meeting together and building each other up, but times will come when that is impossible to achieve. None of us enjoys such times, but we all go through them, whether we are married or single. In fact, anyone who is growing and advancing in God will have to go through at least one personal Gethsemane, if not more.

When your discouragement is profound and you do not seem to have allies, you can do what King David did at Ziklag. Do you remember the story? David and his six hundred men were away from the city, leaving their families defenseless when the Amalekites attacked (see 1 Sam. 30). The Amalekites torched the city and captured all the women and children. When David and his men returned to the smoking ruins, they were distraught:

> Then David and the people who were with him lifted up their voices and wept, until they had no more power to weep. And David's two wives, Ahinoam the Jezreelitess, and Abigail the widow of Nabal the Carmelite, had been taken captive. Now David was greatly distressed, for the people spoke of stoning him, because the soul of all the people was grieved, every man for his sons and his daughters. But David strengthened himself in the Lord his God (1 Samuel 30:4-6).

They wept until they were exhausted. Now what were they going to do? David was just as distressed as the rest of his men, and yet they blamed him. Hadn't he taken them away from the city on his military business so that they were gone when the Amalekites came? They threatened to stone him to death.

Their fury against him only added isolation and fear to David's personal anguish. Forced to his knees, *"David strengthened himself in the Lord his God"* (1 Sam. 30:6). We don't know how he did it, but somehow he turned his attention to God, and essentially prophesied bravery back into himself. "God, this seems hopeless. You must have a plan. Tell me what to do." God did. Next thing they knew, David was leading his men off to rescue their wives and sons and daughters. Already exhausted before they started, about 200 of them could not continue, but 400 men kept tracking their enemies, assisted by a slave of the Amalekites who had been abandoned in a field. They found the enemy camp and attacked it relentlessly until they prevailed, reclaiming their families, not one of whom was lost. They got back their possessions too, multiplied by other prizes of war that the Amalekites had pillaged.

You and I will never have to attack an Amalekite army to rescue our family members, but we will certainly have times when God will seem to remove every prop, every friend, every glimmer of hope. In those times, we are going to find out whether or not we know God. We, too, can strengthen ourselves in the Lord, laying hold of truth from Scripture and song and coming up with ideas that will restore our courage. We may have to reach back across the centuries to recharge our faith with Scripture or other words of faith, but if we turn to Him, God will send us the strength and spiritual bravery we need to conquer our blackest foes.

STIR IT UP

Job could have used a little encouragement. He was sitting in his sackcloth and ashes with sores all over his body, trying to figure out what he did wrong to deserve what had befallen him. Along came his wife. Surely she would give him a kiss and say, "Honey, we are going to be all right; at least we have each other."

But no. Instead it's more like, "Eww. Job, baby, on top of everything else, you have halitosis!" As Job recounted it, *My breath is offensive to my wife*" (Job 19:17). She left the room so fast he couldn't even ask her for a breath mint.

Sometimes we are like Job's friends or his wife. We become so familiar with each other that we look at the evidence and we think we know why our friend is having a hard time. We diagnose and categorize and criticize. But do we take time to listen to the Holy Spirit to see if He has a helpful word for us to share? Do we develop the inclination to say "I bless you, even though I don't understand any better than you do"?

What some of us think is discernment is really only our own human evaluation. We need to push the pause button and stir ourselves up to hear from God on our friend's behalf. We need to keep knocking and looking for a word that is a true word from the Lord.

We need to increase our love and deepen our relationships by means of allowing the Holy Spirit to work in us and through us. Peter wrote, *"Since you have in obedience to the truth purified your souls for a sincere love of the brethren, fervently love one another from the heart"* (1 Pet. 1:22 NASB). Allowing the Holy Spirit to move through me to reach a person in need is one of the greatest joys of my life with Christ. Bringing encouragement to someone's tired heart and imparting bravery to them for the battles they are fighting is more valuable than money.

You may never know the results, but sometimes you will find out what happened as a result of your prophetic outreach. Once I was at some random meeting that I wasn't even supposed to be attending. A man came up to me and said, "You were in Hawaii a number of years ago and I thought my life was over. You gave me a word from the Lord that changed my whole life." I do not remember the occasion, but that does not matter. God knew that man needed a word of encouragement and evidently He used me as His messenger. When a word comes from God, it makes a big difference.

Stir yourself up to allow God's river of love to flow through you to impart so much courage that another person can not only resist difficult circumstances but also overcome them. The writer of Hebrews recommends that we *"Let love of the brethren continue"* (Heb. 13:1 NASB). The word translated "continue" means "increase." And there is no better way for the love between us to increase than for us to keep reaching out to *"strengthen the hands that are weak and the knees that are feeble"* (Heb. 12:12 NASB). Scripture plainly states that you and I are the righteousness of God in Christ Jesus and that nothing can separate us from His love (see 2 Cor. 5:21; Rom. 8:35-39). It also tells us that the Lord who began a good work in you will see it through to completion, which implies that He will supply courage and determination for clearing every hurdle (see Phil. 1:6).

All we need to do is stir ourselves up to make ourselves available to God, so that He can use us to tell good news to hurting people.

Everything Jesus Says

Sometimes I just "read the red" in my Bible, because all of Jesus' words are prophetic. Needless to say, His *rhema* words today are prophetic too, filled with power and authority and restoration. He can't help but prophesy because He is God. He says, "... *The words that I speak to you are spirit, and they are life*" (John 6:63). His words stand immovable in the face of the outrage of the enemy.

You and I are Jesus' disciples. We are supposed to be conformed to His image (see Rom. 8:29). We can live the same life, apparently even doing greater works than He did (see John 14:12).

Sometimes people talk about the evil spirits that control their city as if the spirits have almost the final word about the place. What are they worrying for? There was a serpent in the Garden of Eden before cities were even invented. Why talk so much about the dark side and how bad everything is, as if the glory of God is not increasing at the same time?

The glory of God is increasing. Remind yourself and remind others about that. On the days when you cannot get yourself up in the morning because your vision is so clouded, God will send you someone to tell you that He is still in charge and all-victorious. Relax and let the person prophesy life into you. If you run into someone who is struggling, wait a minute, listening to the Holy Spirit, and then start loving and blessing your friend with what He gives you. What He gives may begin to tap into a vein that touches the person's heart in a way that only God could know. Life will flow. Both of you will understand in a fresh way what being a new creature in Christ feels like. You get revived along with your friend.

This is prophetic encouragement; there is nothing else like it.

Chapter 4

Receiving and Responding to Prophetic Ministry

Mickey Robinson

Five fellow pastors and I, all from local churches in Ohio, started meeting in 1988 to pray together. Our theme was "how to be properly prophetic in these last days." At first, we did not really know each other very well, and none of us realized that what we were doing was part of a move of God across the nation and world. Then we found out that many groups were pursuing the same theme, such as Christian International with Dr. Bill Hamon and Kansas City Fellowship with Mike Bickle and premier radical teammates, and eventually we networked with many of them. In various ways, these other ministries wanted to do the same thing that we did—equip people to use their spiritual gifts, especially the prophetic gifts, in a way that would honor God.

Drawing on each other's streams was a good idea. Of course we found similarities and patterns in the way the Holy Spirit moved through people prophetically, but we also found a divine uniqueness in every person and every group. We all learned from each other and matured as we walked together. One thing we learned most of all: God loves to blend individuals with unique gifts and different backgrounds. Together we can better represent the fullness of God.

Coming into contact with so many different leaders and ministries, I never found any experts, just a lot of really good people who are learners and followers of the Lord Jesus Christ, walking in the adventure together. I never want to become an expert, either. (After all, an "ex" is a has-been and a "spurt" is a drip under pressure!) I just want to be a person who is hungrier today than I was yesterday. I know that God has more to give us than anybody has yet to receive and I want to receive everything He wants to give me in this lifetime.

SEED TO FRUIT

I think all of us should feel this way—desiring everything possible from God—because each of us has the Holy Spirit inside us, and when you have the Holy Spirit in you, nothing is left out. You have the full magnitude of God in you. You don't have the junior Holy Spirit. You have all the ingredients. You've got healing; you've got deliverance; you've got teaching; you've got administration, and so on. And you have prophecy.

Much has been written and taught about ministering prophetically, and a lot of the teaching has been illustrated with dramatic stories about how somebody very accurately told a person his name, age, favorite color, and what kind of healing he needs. I love those stories, because you can see God's fingerprints on them, but they do not represent a very high percentage of prophetic activity.

I think it is more important to know how to respond properly to God the Holy Spirit in all kinds of prophetic situations. (By the way, in case you didn't know it, the Holy Spirit really is under the impression that He is God. We need to learn how to respond to Him, because it's true—He *is* God.) We need to be able to see what the word of the Lord is revealing, regardless of the package the message comes in, and we need to know how to watch over His words so that they can come to fulfillment and yield a harvest of fruit.

WHAT KIND OF FRUIT?

The often-repeated purpose of prophetic ministry is worth reiterating in this context. The purpose of prophetic ministry is to edify (build up) people, exhort and encourage people, and comfort people. The foundational Scripture is this one: *"But he who prophesies speaks edification and exhortation and comfort to men"* (1 Cor. 14:3). Edification, exhortation, and comfort reflect the nature of God's love.

To edify people means to build them up spiritually, emotionally, and morally, to bring them into greater freedom and greater health. Instead of being like Job's comforters, telling people they have something wrong with them and that it must be their fault, we tap into God's inexhaustible supply of love to lift them to new levels.

Exhorting people is not the same as browbeating them. It means to persuade, encourage, implore, and entreat. Exhortation can include admonishment or warning. Sometimes it will be directive. But you must realize that even admonishment and warning are positive things, because they keep you from harm. God uses prophetic means to influence, lead, guide, and protect us.

So we are looking for prophetic words that bring the fruit of the Kingdom of God into human lives. We are on the lookout for God's encouragement, strengthening, protection, maturing, freedom, health, provision, guidance, and all other expressions of His fatherly love.

PRAYERS ANSWERED, PROPHECIES FULFILLED

Prophecy is never prophecy until it is fulfilled. God is never glorified until prayers are answered. Do these sound like extreme statements? They are biblical. Jesus said, "By this My Father is glorified, that you bear much fruit" (John 15:8). And earlier, Isaiah wrote:

> *For as the rain comes down, and the snow from Heaven, and*
> *do not return there, but water the earth, and make it bring*

forth and bud, that it may give seed to the sower and bread to the eater, so shall My word be that goes forth from My mouth; it shall not return to Me void, but it shall accomplish what I please, and it shall prosper in the thing for which I sent it (Isaiah 55:10-11).

God's word will bear fruit. It will accomplish what He intends, sooner or later. Even when God speaks to someone and that person hears it but never follows through with it, somebody else will follow through with it. A true word from God is not going back to Him without somebody fulfilling it, even if it takes a long time.

Have you ever met a person and you feel as if you have known them for a thousand years? This does not have anything to do with reincarnation. When that happens, it is because that person is carrying the same burden of the Lord that somebody has been carrying for a thousand years, still awaiting fulfillment. The person you just met represents another opportunity for God's word or action to be expressed and received. The person is carrying God's heart's desire.

God is always looking for someone to satisfy His desires. God does not give prophecies to people just so they will feel good. He wants something to happen. He has a specific purpose that He wants to have fulfilled.

But His purposes can be thwarted. Prophecy is conditional. People can mess it up. They can drop the ball. They can delay or derail an important part of God's plan for their lives and for others.

Some people doubt and reject prophetic ministry because of mistakes, abuses, or immaturity, which means that God's word has been neglected again and again. Paul spoke to his son-in-faith, Timothy:

This charge I commit to you, son Timothy, according to the prophecies previously made concerning you, that by them you may wage the good warfare, having faith and a good conscience, which some having rejected, concerning the faith have suffered shipwreck (1 Timothy 1:18-19).

"This charge I commit to you"—that is persuasive and it is directive—that you fulfill the prophetic words that were spoken over you by fighting the good fight with faith and a good conscience, not like some people. In other words, those other people had a prophetic destiny too. But after they received the words about them, they said to themselves, *Now I am going to just do whatever I want to do.* They rejected the word of the Lord.

Although they recognized true words from God, they didn't realize that the words that came to them were in seed form and that they might have to nurture and cultivate them before they would come to pass.

RECEPTIVE AND RESPONSIVE

Through His servant, the prophet Amos, God said, *"Surely the Lord God does nothing unless He reveals His secret counsel to His servants the prophets"* (Amos 3:7 NASB). That is an amazing statement. Evidently, God does not do anything without first telling a human being who is able to hear what His Spirit is saying. The prophet does not need to be well-known. God could tell something to some homeschooling mom, and she prays for it to happen or shouts it out the window or writes it down in her journal. He could reveal His secret counsel to you or to me.

When God reveals His secret counsel, His word might not concern something big like world peace or even the next hurricane in the Caribbean. It may be a simple word of direction about a personal decision or a slight nudge to pay attention to the weather. But any word from God is more important than CNN (which I think must mean "Constantly Negative News"). Any word from God is significant because it reveals His desires.

Amos' next line is more poetic, and it is loaded with meaning: *"A lion has roared! Who will not fear? The Lord God has spoken! Who can but prophesy?"* (Amos 3:8 NASB). When the king of the pride, the dominant male lion, roars with his mighty voice, all of his enemies cringe. In the same way, when God speaks through one of His servants, that word comes out of that servant into the atmosphere, energizing the earth with the prophetic word of God.

When a human being speaks, everybody knows that it is just a person, but when God speaks through that human, he or she becomes a yielded vessel for the word of the Lord. That word, even if it is brief, reverberates in the heavens. It is the voice of the Lord. His enemies cringe, but those who are His own children know they are safe and secure in His everlasting love.

Earnestly Desire

It is no small thing to hear from the God of the Universe. Why do we take His words so lightly and even forget about them?

The Bible tells us to drop everything in favor of hearing from God. Paul wrote a letter to the church in Corinth and he said, *"Brethren, desire earnestly to prophesy..."* (1 Cor. 14:39). He was repeating what he had just said a few lines earlier: *"Pursue love, yet desire earnestly spiritual gifts, but especially that you may prophesy"* (1 Cor. 14:1 NASB). All of us are supposed to really, *really* want to hear from God. It's not a suggestion or an invitation—it is imperative, a command.

Through another one of his Old Testament prophets, Joel, God said:

> It shall come to pass afterward that I will pour out My Spirit on all flesh; your sons and your daughters shall prophesy, your old men shall dream dreams, your young men shall see visions. And also on My menservants and on My maidservants I will pour out My Spirit in those days (Joel 2:28-29).

That word does not say, "You will all prophesy...if it be My will," or "I will pour out my Spirit on a few privileged people who have long titles after their names." It says "I will pour out My Spirit on *all flesh*," and all people *shall* prophesy. Joel was foreseeing the future. Today, each and every one of us has an obligation to respond to the outpouring of the Holy Spirit because we are living in the midst of it.

We should have an ever-increasing level of expectancy. We should learn how to tune in to His voice and we should learn what to do when we hear it. What does He mean? How will His word affect us? Sometimes it takes us awhile to get it, but we should be pursuing God's word all the time.

There is nothing more important than what God is saying or doing or intending at a particular juncture of time, yet people do not even know the basics of how to hear and interpret what He wants. The only remedy is to turn away from apathy and earthly limitations and to ask Him to open our spiritual ears to hear and understand Him.

THE REVERBERATING WORD

If God is not speaking, there is no order in the created cosmos. He holds everything together by the sustaining power of His word (see Heb. 1:3). The cosmos includes every created thing, whether we can see it with our eyes or not—every electron, every star, every galaxy.

This is the God who urges us to seek after His word:

> God, who at various times and in various ways spoke in time past to the fathers by the prophets, has in these last days spoken to us by His Son, whom He has appointed heir of all things… (Hebrews 1:1-2).

And the fullness of the power of His Son's Spirit is dwelling in you and me. Paul again:

> Beware lest anyone cheat you through philosophy and empty deceit, according to the tradition of men, according to the basic principles of the world, and not according to Christ. For in Him dwells all the fullness of the Godhead bodily; and

*you are complete in Him, who is the head of all principality
and power* (Colossians 2:8-10).

The same God who parted the Red Sea is in you. The same God who
spoke to Noah before the Flood is in you. The God who did all that we read
in the Bible is inside of you, and He wants out. He wants to express Himself
through your life.

God's creative word is still reverberating throughout the universe. A
while back, scientists discovered that there is something in the ever-ex-
panding universe that they called "background noise." Wouldn't that be
the voice of God, reverberating, "Let there be light"? Galaxies and earth
with all the life delicately placed on it—His Word is sustaining it all.

Wouldn't it also make sense that God's voice would become audible to
the spiritual ears of His children, in whom His Spirit dwells?

LEARNING TO RESPOND TO THE HOLY SPIRIT

Our responsibility to respond to the Holy Spirit does not imply that
each one of us should have an active gift of prophecy. You don't have to
be a prophet in such a time as this, when the spirit of prophecy is being
released. So many of our songs release the testimony of Jesus, and so much
of our intercession picks up on His heart's desires.

When you are singing prophetic songs that accurately portray the will
of God, you are in a prophetic atmosphere. That is not the time to say, "Excuse me, God, you have to be quiet; we're busy singing our songs." It is the
time to learn how to respond to the Holy Spirit.

FAITH IS THE FOUNDATION

You cannot receive the word of God without faith. Oftentimes it is the
revelatory word itself that sparks the faith necessary to receive it. The spirit
of revelation itself ignites something supernatural and faith just rises up.

Suddenly you can simply believe that God can do whatever He just said, even if it seems ridiculous or impossible.

Take, for example, raising the dead. Normally we don't expect to be able to do that. It is quite a step up from healing. And yet raising the dead is part of the Gospel message, and we should be open to doing it if that is what God wants to do. I have never done it yet, but I know people who have done it multiple times.

I have prayed for four people who were in vegetative comas, when there was really no medical prognosis of having a quality life ever again, and they all woke up with no brain damage. That is pretty exciting. One of them was an orthodox Jewish woman. She pulled the tubes out of her nose, sat up in bed, and gave her heart to Jesus. Her parents had brought us to the Chicago hospital where she was a patient. There was absolutely no hope. Her eyes were fixed and dilated, none of her organs worked, and she was hooked up to all kinds of machines. We anointed her with oil, and she groaned. A man was whispering the Gospel into her ear and I began to command certain things. Do you think we had a gift of faith and that it prevailed over what we could see? We trusted the word of the Lord and He fulfilled it.

Faith is foundational; *"faith is the substance of things hoped for, the evidence of things not seen"* (Heb. 11:1). Every building needs some kind of a foundation, something solid on which to build the rest of the structure. Faith is the substance that gets laid down first before the delivery and building and working-out of a prophetic word.

Before anything else happens, somebody has a revelation and their faith explodes—*this is going to happen, even though it does not exist yet*—and the seed of the prophetic word gets planted in good soil. This faith bypasses the human intellect, which can be a major barrier to receptivity in the spiritual realm. It makes the impossible possible. Preconceived ideas are reduced to rubble when the lion of God roars.

EAGER ACCEPTANCE

Once faith takes root in our hearts, receptivity to the word of the Lord is not much of a problem—or at least it should not be. In actual fact, a person's eager acceptance of the word is all-important. The Holy Spirit has sparked a word inside someone and instantly they must make a choice. To receive or not to receive? To believe or not?

It is all too easy to *quench* the Spirit or *grieve* the Spirit (see 1 Thess. 5:19; Eph. 4:30). Or you can eagerly *embrace* whatever He has chosen to send you (see 1 Thess. 2:13).

Many people, thinking that they are being sensible, say, "Well, let's just wait and see. I'm not buying into a word from God just because someone else does." This shows that they are slow of heart and not eager to receive what God wants to do. They would prefer to have the Holy Spirit blast into their hearts with a jackhammer, but He will not do that. He is looking for hearts that are soft and pliable and sensitive to Him. He may allow you to go through a crisis to help you get there, but His goal is to make you able to sense the slightest thing that God is doing.

The nature of your receptivity is up to you, but you will always have some kind of an initial response when God speaks. Here are your three options: (1) you can totally reject the word, miss the word, or fight against it; (2) you can be passive about it; or (3) you can listen to it and commit your way to it. When you choose the first option, you come up with something that is opposite to the word and you challenge the word or cancel it out. When you are passive, you do not exert yourself in any direction, even a negative one. But the end result is negative because the word drops in a void instead of getting planted in your heart.

When God speaks a "now" word, it transcends the temporal world. You need to learn how to live out of the eternal realm instead of the natural world because your real self is a spirit and you have everlasting life now. Learn how to stop taking all of your cues from what you can discover with your five natural senses and start taking your cues from what God is doing.

Allow the prophetic word to break down your intellectual barriers and your resulting resistance to receptivity. Allow the word of the Lord to form patterns in your heart and also in your mind. Remember that the word of the Lord is often in seed form, but the seed holds the pattern of the mature plant. (An acorn is small enough for squirrels to carry around and eat, but it carries the final pattern for a massive oak tree.)

The pattern of your prophetic destiny is contained in a short prophetic word. If you receive it and allow it to be sown into you, it can develop and grow. Don't stop with eagerness or excitement over the initial word. The result of your initial receptivity should be implantation and growth. Let the process begin!

TEST IT

As soon as you hear a word, you begin to test it. I try not to use the word "judge," but that is the biblical word for it. "Let two or three prophets speak, and let the others judge" (1 Cor. 14:29).

What the word "judge" means is to sort out and separate and see what's there (not so much deciding whether the word is from God, the devil, or the flesh). You discern. Does your spirit bear witness to the entire word or to part of it? Does it have the fingerprints of God on it? Do other people's spirits bear witness to it, especially other prophetic people? Is it consistent with Scripture? Have you noticed other kinds of confirmations, such as "coincidental" circumstances?

In the church I pastored in Ohio, we permitted corporate prophecy on Sundays. Every week my secretary transcribed the recorded prophecies and published them on the back of the next Sunday's bulletin. We wanted people to be able to discern them. Having made room for prophecy in the weekly service (which I think should be the norm in a church), we wanted to follow through and allow people to consider the words, give feedback, and decide what they were supposed to do with them.

Whatever you do, do not spurn or deride the prophetic ministry or individual prophecies. Paul wrote, *"Do not despise prophecies"* (1 Thess. 5:20). Don't write them off wholesale. ("I don't know about those stupid prophecies and I don't want to hear any more of them." "I don't like the way that person does it, and I'll just ignore what he says.") If a word seems controversial or the delivery is unusual, keep looking for the fingerprints of God and just disregard the messy container that the word came in. Or, as people often say, "Take the meat and spit out the bones." Over the years you will hear false prophecy, bad prophecy, and fleshly prophecy, but do not let that make you throw the baby out with the bathwater. Testing, judging, and discerning prophecy is like a detective looking for the forensic fingerprints and DNA of God. When we get it we say, "Yes! I knew it was Him."

You should not be naïve and accept everything uncritically, but you do not have to be overly analytical. Line your own heart up with God's to find out His opinion about a word. He speaks all over the world through all kinds of people, and He wants us to pay attention to what He is saying.

Watch Out for the Vision Robber

As you are learning to test prophetic words, be alert for a spiritual dynamic that can rob you of the truth of the word. Sometimes, immediately after a prophetic word is released, every mind-blowing, earthshaking, gut-wrenching thing can happen. The wind seems to start blowing in the opposite direction.

Just hang in there until you can see that word fulfilled. You have probably heard the statement, "higher levels, higher devils." I prefer to believe that the higher the spiritual level, the higher the angels. You may tell yourself, "Well, I must be doing something right because the devil is really hassling me." I prefer to say, "If I'm doing something right, *he* is going to get hassled. I am going to overcome him." Just press forward and get on with it.

Occasionally, of course, God fulfills a word immediately. But more often, God allows a space of time between the delivery of a word and its fulfillment so that we can develop the necessary personal character and so that certain elements can come together.

Sometimes you will need to continue confessing a prophetic word, even singing or speaking it out. I remember a couple in California. They couldn't have children and they got prayed for. They were anointed with oil and prophesied over. People kept having dreams and visions that they were going to have a child, but nothing happened. Some people even gave them baby clothes. Then they read, *"Sing, O barren one"* in Isaiah 54:1 (AMP), and they followed through by walking through their house, prophetically singing about their child out of the brokenness of their hearts. It released something. Next thing we heard, the wife got pregnant and she delivered a healthy baby.

Some prophetic seeds are planted in a resting season. They endure the "winter" and then they begin to sprout. Breakthrough occurs. Timing, circumstances, people, resources begin to come together. That is not the fulfillment, not yet. The prophetic word is starting to come into being, but it is not done yet. When that happens, don't run ahead of God to try to make things happen. Just pray and participate. You need to prepare for the purposes of God, recognizing the signs of progress and blessing the evidences of God's work.

CULTIVATE THE WORD

To extend the metaphor of the prophetic word as a seed, it is as if you need to cultivate the word that has been planted and that is beginning to grow. You need to apply wisdom and faith and the anointing of God to it.

When our prophetic team first came together, we felt that God wanted us to operate in a way that would highlight two words—"faith," and "unity."

We even put it into our bylaws that we were going to enjoy friendship with one another and that we were going to have fun together. So besides praying together, we went out to eat together, we went to shows together, and we played golf together (and I didn't even like golf).

Becoming such a cohesive team was part of our cultivation of the prophetic ministry. I know this because many times we would receive some of our best strategy in a quick 20 minutes after we had been playing together, singing, telling jokes, and so forth. The anointing of God would come down and we would produce plans that we could not have thought up on our own, faster than we could have done it on our own.

Another aspect of cultivation is repetition. You don't hoe your vegetable garden just once. You keep doing it. You practice the exercise of the prophetic gift, and you become better at it. You practice hearing God, discerning His words, and putting them into practice. Cultivation leads to maturity.

BEARING FRUIT

Eventually, the prophetic word *will* bear fruit. Here again, it can happen suddenly, or it can be a very gradual process. You may become part of a new church or shift your ministry emphasis or enter into a new alliance with others and explosive growth bursts forth. Or, years later, you may re-read something you wrote in your journal and understand it in a whole new light because you have walked it out.

One prophetic word may bear more fruit than you expected. A farmer does not take a kernel of corn and walk all over his farm looking for the ideal spot to plant it, anticipating one corn plant. He broadcasts lots of kernels, covering as much of the ground as he can, and when those seeds sprout and grow into mature stalks, each stalk will bear three or four ears. On each ear of corn there are hundreds of kernels, each with the potential to reproduce more than a hundredfold.

In other words, prophetic fruit will bear more fruit. The planting that you labored over has the potential to multiply greatly. Your one prophetic word can touch hundreds or thousands of people.

God is never satisfied nor is He glorified until you bear fruit and your fruit remains. Jesus said:

> *I am the vine, you are the branches. He who abides in Me, and I in him, bears much fruit; for without Me you can do nothing. ...By this My Father is glorified, that you bear much fruit.... You did not choose Me, but I chose you and appointed you that you should go and bear fruit, and that your fruit should remain...* (John 15:5,8,16).

Fruitfulness is the ultimate hallmark of someone who receives and responds to the prophetic ministry of the Holy Spirit through one of God's servants who is a prophet. And divine fruit will last forever.

PART TWO

RELEVANT DEMONSTRATIONS OF THE PROPHETIC TODAY

Stand on tiptoe as you read the next few chapters, because they will stretch your perspective on the prophetic. First up is a chapter by the adventuresome founder of a ministry called Extreme Prophetic, who will expand your perspective on how the prophetic gifts bring Kingdom justice to some of the most hopeless situations in the world.

The next chapter will broaden your horizons into the realm of God's glory as you are drawn beyond the familiar natural world to see how you can connect your spirit with His Spirit for the sake of discerning and releasing a supernatural flow of prophetic revelation from the heavenly realm.

Then you will find a chapter by Michal Ann Goll, who has graduated to the realm of glory herself, but who, when she was still with us, opened many doorways into the adventure of prophetic intercession. We are the connectors between the realm of earth and the realm of God's Kingdom, and her chapter shows us how we can learn from the Holy Spirit to use the prophetic keys that He has given us.

Chapter 5

THE PROPHETIC AND JUSTICE

Patricia King

When I was newly born again, a woman in our church in Canada prophesied over me. As the words poured forth from her mouth, I remember how it felt to have my soul flooded with the tangible love of Jesus. I was so strongly aware of His presence, it was as if Jesus Himself were speaking to me, not her. The words He spoke were profoundly affirming and encouraging, and they ignited an intense, burning, passionate response within me. I had never before experienced such a response for anyone or anything.

In a glorious way, that prophetic word revealed the Lord's heart to me. Immediately, it drew me deeper into relationship with Him. I felt so safe in His love, and as a result I wanted to know Him more. I pursued Him to the point of becoming completely absorbed in seeking Him. One taste of His deep and powerful love can be addictive! I became a true *Jesus-love-addict*.

After that experience, I received many other prophetic words from various people in our church. Every prophetic utterance had the same effect on me. All of them expressed His love in such tender ways. Each word edified, exhorted, and comforted me, and they always made me hungry for more of Him.

At first, I had no idea that the prophetic gift was available to every believer. After awhile, however, one of the prophetically fluent women in our church invited me to attend a training school led by her mentor, Mary Goddard. I was more than excited, and I eagerly accepted the invitation. At the ten-day training school, I learned about the gifts of the Spirit, and I "learned" how to prophesy. That is right, I learned to hear the voice of God and to proclaim what He revealed.

The training was foundational and it made a powerful impact on me, especially because the way we learned to activate the gift was by prophesying over each other. I found it very exciting to wait on the Lord, receive a word by faith, and then deliver it. I so wanted to see others encouraged in the way I had been. The classes were fun and the Holy Spirit always blessed us with His presence and power.

Our mentor, Mary (who has since gone on to be with the Lord), encouraged us always to be "prayed up" and ready to receive a word of prophetic blessing for other people. She said, "Take every opportunity to prophesy," so I did just that.

After the training school, I would spend at least an hour a day (which usually became three or more hours) praying in tongues. Then I would spend extra time in prayer before attending a Bible study, prayer meeting, or church service. I learned to invite the Holy Spirit to use me as an instrument of His love, as His voice.

When there was an opportunity in the meetings, I would bring forth inspired revelatory words. Every opportunity I got, I would prophesy. No one left our home without a prophetic blessing. I loved waiting on the Lord for His words for people, and I loved to see them touched.

EVERLASTING LOVE

One Sunday morning prior to the commencement of our church service, a friend of mine met me in the foyer and said, "Hey, Patricia, I know what you are going to prophesy this morning." I was both shocked and amazed at how profoundly prophetic he must be to actually know ahead of time what word of the Lord I would bring.

I said, "You're kidding! What am I going to prophesy?" I didn't know myself, yet.

Confidently, he replied, "You will say something like, 'God loves you with an everlasting love.'"

Again I was amazed. I asked him how he knew (thinking that perhaps the Lord had revealed this to him in a dream or through an audible voice). He chuckled and explained, "I don't have to be prophetic to know this. I know it because every Sunday for the past nine months you have said almost the same prophetic word. It is always about how God loves us with an unfailing and eternal and everlasting love."

I had no idea I was bringing the same word every Sunday! To me, it was always fresh. I had continued to prepare for Sunday mornings by being "prayed up," and I had tried to remain attentive to hear what the Spirit was saying so that I could encourage the body of Christ. My exercise of the prophetic gift was very simple, and it was valid in spite of the repetitiveness.

Since then, I have come to realize that the prophetic word that I delivered for so many months—"God loves you with an everlasting love"—is probably the most profound and powerful word that can possibly come from the heart of God. That word is for all people and for all time.

As time went on, I began to receive a variety of specific words, but I must admit that the core message **I continue to this day to carry for the Lord** remains that same word about God's love. I teach a training course called Prophetic Bootcamp. Part of the training is activation. Often, students feel very nervous because they are afraid that they will not receive a word from God when they are supposed to. In order to give them some backup support, I tell them, "If you find that your fear makes you freeze up emotionally and you feel brain-dead, here is a prophetic word that you can pull out. In times of trouble, it is a powerful word. It is meant for all people and for all time: *"God loves you with an everlasting love...He really* *does!*" After that, most students can relax enough to hear God clearly on their own.

Our prophetic evangelism activation classes go out directly to the streets. Many times they have returned from the streets rejoicing because they used this word to good effect. Having drawn a blank in the middle of a witnessing encounter, they simply said, "God loves you with an everlasting love...He really does!" They testify, "It works! The person was touched so deeply that he even cried when I told him that God loves him with an everlasting love."

God Loves—and God Hates

It is very important for us to understand the love of God, because He *is* love. He loves you and He loves me. He loves *all* people, all the time:

> For God so loved the world that He gave His only begotten Son, that whoever believes in Him should not perish but have everlasting life (John 3:16).

He does not love us only when we are well-behaved, obedient, and compliant children, although He really enjoys it when we are. He loves us also when we are rebelling against Him: *"...While we were still sinners, Christ died for us"* (Rom. 5:8).

Be assured, God loves you and He will never withdraw His love. Jesus proved this by passing every love-test during His earthly ministry. Faced with people's rebellion, disobedience, betrayal, denial, abandonment, and cruelty, He laid down His life for us. He died on the Cross for us so that we could have His righteousness. We were still His enemies when He did that.

This God-love is amazing and nearly impossible to understand, and yet it is real and it is true. Jesus became sin so that we could become His righteousness (see 2 Cor. 5:21). He became poor so that we could become rich (see 2 Cor. 8:9). Nothing we can do can make Him withdraw His love from us. His love is perfect and His love is eternal.

God's prophetic word to us will always reflect His love for humankind. The spirit of prophecy is the testimony of Jesus (see Rev. 19:10). New Testament prophecy represents the heart of God's love for us, and it is fulfilled in Christ's finished work of the Cross.

Scripture teaches us clearly what love looks like and what it acts like:

> *Love is patient, love is kind and is not jealous; love does not brag and is not arrogant, does not act unbecomingly; it does not seek its own, is not provoked, does not take into account a wrong suffered, does not rejoice in unrighteousness, but rejoices with the truth; bears all things, believes all things, hopes all things, endures all things. Love never fails...* (1 Corinthians 13:4-8 NASB).

Clearly, God (who is love) does not rejoice in unrighteousness, but rather He rejoices with the truth.

At the same time—and this is equally important—God hates sin with a perfect hatred. God actually demonstrates wrath against all unrighteousness and the ungodliness of men (see Rom. 1:18). Sin pits itself against God's love, so He opposes it utterly.

Let me explain with this example. Let's say a rapist is targeting a community and he has already sexually assaulted three young women with violence. If you truly love, you will hate the sin of rape and you will want the rapist caught, arrested, and punished so that the community will be free from further attacks. You will also want the rapist to be protected from committing further offenses. This is justice in action—wise action will bring forth divine alignment with the plumb line of God's love.

The heart of love has no room for affection or even tolerance for the act of rape. The heart of love hates rape because it hurts people. In the same way, all sin hurts people; that is why God hates it so much.

Scripture says that the devil is the father of lies but that Jesus is Truth (see John 8:44; 14:6). Love always rejoices when the truth wins out. Spirit-inspired prophecy always represents the truth. Therefore, prophecy is God's voice of love and God's voice of truth.

God is the ultimate Lover, and the Church is His Bride. His Bride hears His voice. She speaks His words to lost people when He tells her to do so, in order to set them free from darkness. Freed from the hold of darkness, they can be added to His Church where they, too, can hear His voice, further enhancing the beauty of the Bride in the eyes of her Lord and Bridegroom, Jesus.

In these days, I believe that the Bride of Christ has begun to prepare a wedding gown for herself that is so spotlessly pure with righteous acts that it can reflect the love of the Bridegroom. Impelled by a greater revelation of the love of His heart, the Bride of Christ will begin to act and look more like Him, and that love will take her into situations of darkness that would have been unimaginable to her before. Her righteous, prophetic acts will bring the blinding light of glory into hearts of people who have never had a chance to glimpse it before, carrying the abundant love of God into places of destitution.

As her righteous acts increase, His Bride will begin to participate in the love of the Bridegroom to such an extent that she will lay down her life as He did on the Cross. When He walked the earth, He said, "Greater love has no one than this, than to lay down one's life for his friends. You are My friends if you do whatever I command you" (John 15:13-14). We are His friends when we hear His voice and obey Him.

RIGHTEOUSNESS, JUSTICE, AND THE PROPHETIC

God's prophetic voice is always righteous. That means that His voice is everything *right*. It is right for people to be healed and set free. It is right for every person God has created to have enough food and provision each day so that they can live comfortably. It is right that children be tucked into bed at night. It is right for all people to be safe. It is right for everybody to be healthy, strong, and joyful. It is right for each person to be morally pure.

Living in the atmosphere of "right" is like living in the atmosphere of Heaven. In Heaven, righteousness and justice are the foundations of His throne (see Ps. 89:14). When righteousness is challenged, attacked, and threatened, then we need justice to restore righteousness.

What does "justice" consist of? Merriam-Webster's dictionary defines justice as:

1a: the maintenance or administration of what is just especially by the impartial adjustment of conflicting claims or the assignment of merited rewards or punishments

1b: judge

1c: the administration of law; especially: the establishment or determination of rights according to the rules of law or equity

2a: the quality of being just, impartial, or fair

2b: (1): the principle or ideal of just dealing or right action (2): conformity to this principle or ideal: righteousness (3): the quality of conforming to law

3: conformity to truth, fact, or reason: correctness

In other words, when anything is out of righteous alignment, the function of justice is to bring it back into righteous alignment. Without justice, unrighteousness will run rampant and destroy innocent people. God's prophetic voice is both righteous and just, and this spells L-O-V-E. God is righteous and He wants us to pursue righteousness day in and day out.

THE PROPHETIC TRUMPET OF JUSTICE

God has called me and the people in my ministry to extend His righteous justice to people whose lives have been the most grievously shattered by evil. From the beginning of my life as a Christian, I was motivated by a driving passion for evangelism. For years, I reached out to the lost in any way I could find to do it, to the point that my routine practice was to undertake some form of evangelistic outreach every single day. Sometimes traveling with my husband Ron, family, and friends, I had many adventures in far northern Canada, Mexico, and many other places.

Our home church in British Columbia, Canada, became a vital center for prophetic ministry. Within the context of church meetings as well as outside, we were free to develop prophetically. About ten years ago, I began to become challenged and convinced that more of us needed to take the prophetic to the malls and cafes and streets—and more. We could see that God had prepared us for new strategies and that He was taking us into places that only the "extreme prophetic" (**which ended up being the name of a media and evangelism department in my ministry**) could penetrate.

The Lord awakened my heart to the injustice of those exploited in the sex trade through a young woman I met a number of years ago in the inner city of Vancouver, British Columbia. "Nicole" had grown up in the foster home system, and while I support and affirm the foster home system as a true mission field with many very good caregivers, this young woman had not been placed in safe homes. Her youth had been spent moving from one foster home to another, and in many of the homes she had experienced physical, emotional, and even sexual abuse.

Nicole decided to run away when she was 12 years of age and she ended up in Vancouver's inner city, where a pimp saw her potential to make him money. He promised to take care of her. He got her addicted to drugs and sent her out to make a living as a street prostitute. She turned her first trick before her thirteenth birthday. She remained trapped in this lifestyle for over 12 years without rescue and without ever hearing the Gospel of love and justice.

When I heard this woman's testimony—she was gloriously saved and is now serving the Lord—I was deeply touched. However, her story haunted me night after night, and it still does. Every time I would think of that confused, lonely, hurting little girl who had known so much hate and abuse, I would groan within. It was a groan of pain, a groan of intercession. *How many other Nicoles are out there?* I wondered. *Who will be a voice for them?* I pondered the questions and then groaned some more.

As my groans echoed the groans of the Spirit, I felt that I had been introduced to a dimension of the Lord's heart that I did not know about. He, too, wept over them and desired to see them loved and set free. What did He want me to do about this?

At that time, the Lord put a trumpet to my lips. He invited me to blow a prophetic trumpet that would rally the Body of Christ together to help exploited children. Since then, my ministry has prophesied this call on television, over the Internet, through books and articles, and most of all through helping them directly.

The prophetic word of the Lord can be expressed in many ways. At times, it is as if the Lord picks us up like a paintbrush and paints a glorious message from His heart on the canvas of our lives. Sometimes the Lord wants us to paint a prophetic picture through mobilization and action. This was one of those situations.

Responding to the call of the Lord's heart, we have reached out to children thrown on garbage heaps, we have facilitated the rescue of child soldiers, we have delivered women and children out of the sex trade, and we have supported organizations that are committed to stopping human trafficking. Why have we tried to do such difficult things? Because our righteous Lord told us to and because it is *right!* The prophetic trumpet of justice sounds clearly, compelling things that are not right to become right, and decreeing the consequences. This is love in action, and it is prophetic.

Not only have we facilitated the rescue of women and children, but we have also decreed the consequences to those who perpetrate the injustice. Prophetic justice involves sounding the alarm of warning—"This is unjust! Repent of this injustice!"—so that mercy can be shown to the penitent. The blood of Christ is so powerful that even the vilest sinner, if truly repentant, can find forgiveness, mercy, and a new life.

ONE REVELATION AWAY FROM KNOWING JESUS

During my first trip into a sex tourism destination in Bangkok, I saw an older man, probably in his late fifties, with a young girl he had purchased for the weekend. She appeared to be in her late teens. They sat across from us in a restaurant. I could see the sadness in the girl's eyes, although she was forcing a smile. Anger rose up in me, and a strong judgment manifested in my emotions against the man she was with. I truly wanted to call fire to come down from Heaven to consume him. I was repulsed by everything he stood for.

To my surprise, the Spirit of the Lord spoke within my spirit, convicting me. This was not the kind of justice He was looking for. He reminded me that *"the anger of man does not achieve the righteousness of God"* (James 1:20 NASB). He then proceeded to reveal to me the pain in the man's life that had caused him to resort to spending a weekend with a young prostitute. My heart melted as the Lord revealed His heart to me concerning both the man and the young bar girl he had purchased for two nights and days. The situation was just plain wrong, yet God loved each of them so deeply. More than righteous anger, the situation required divine alignment. If both of them could encounter the living Jesus, they would be convicted, convinced, and helped by the love of God to start walking on a straight path.

The most wicked person in the universe is only one revelation away from knowing Jesus. When salvation comes, alignment with His righteousness will happen.

That evening, we did not have the privilege of leading those two to the Lord, but since then we have led many in that part of the world to Jesus. They are all victims—the prostitutes as well as those who buy them. They are being exploited by the devil's agenda and purposes. They all need to be rescued. Outside of the powerful reach of God, they are hopelessly mired in the darkness of sin.

Through the supernatural power of prophetic evangelism, they can be led to Jesus and rescued from any aspect of the sex trade. Through dedicated believers who rely on God's ability to make wrongs right, they can be placed in sound, loving, and credible discipleship environments. Right now, many of these people are completely out of the sex trade and serving the Lord with all their hearts. They have stepped into their heavenly destiny, which has been prophesied over them by words and actions. They have been able to come into alignment with the righteousness of God. This is justice in action.

PROPHETIC STRATEGIES

While in Pattaya, Thailand, during a scouting trip, we joined one of the local ministry's outreaches into the bars. It was Valentine's Day and the ministry that was hosting us had offered the bars "free entertainment" for this special occasion. The entertainment consisted of singing love songs right in the bar.

As the "Jesus love songs" filled the darkness of the bars, a fresh breath of Heaven came in. Righteousness invaded the unrighteous atmosphere. We also gave words of knowledge and prophetic words publicly, calling individuals forward to receive prophetic ministry. Before long, we had a line of girls waiting for their prophetic words. Through this bold prophetic evangelism, prostitutes were coming to Christ as they learned about God's destiny and purposes for their lives. It was glorious to see Christ's light invading the darkness.

Since that initial visit, our ministry has returned to that region many times, teaching about prophetic evangelism and activating it. We have prophesied the heart of God's rich love and righteousness in the bars, brothels, AIDS hospices, and strip clubs. We have delivered the word of the Lord to prostitutes, transvestites, orphans, prisoners, slum-dwellers, bar and brothel owners, and sex tourists. We have seen powerful results as the prophetic word has influenced lives for righteousness and justice.

JANIE

"Janie" was 14 years of age, but she looked like she was about 8. Reduced to skin and bones, she was dying of AIDS. In her short life, she had known only pain, horrific abuse, and loneliness. She was obviously demonized, her eyes dark with fear and bondage.

A Christian worker found her and brought her to the AIDS hospice where she was loved and cared for. During our time with her, she was initially withdrawn and not at all open to receiving salvation. Our team continued to love her, and eventually she opened up like a beautiful flower right before our eyes.

We prayed and prophesied over her and led her to Jesus. She was gloriously delivered that same day. Her eyes cleared and we literally watched the fear leave as joy filled her face. All of us were weeping with the tears of God's heart of compassion.

Once again, the prophetic trumpet call for justice had brought someone into the Kingdom. Another dear child of God had been snatched from the abusive grip of the enemy. Again righteousness had prevailed over unrighteousness and justice had prevailed over deeply-rooted injustice.

We prayed for Janie's healing. Our worker visited her frequently, and she would hold Janie and sing over her. She brought gifts—cuddle toys and a pair of brand new shoes (of a favorite type that Janie had always wanted). Eventually, Janie went on to be with the Lord, but her last days were filled with joy and peace. She was adored and beautifully cared for in an environment that was saturated with love. Day by day, the prophetic song of her eternal destiny in Christ filled her heart, mind, and body. The Lord's presence was tangible to her through the caring commitment of those around her.

The more Janie experienced the glory of her loving Father in her final days on earth, the more she wanted to go home to be with Him. One day, her heart's desire won out—and she went. Janie is now experiencing the ultimate measure of righteousness and justice, and she will never have to experience any abuse, pain, or sickness again.

WILL SOMEONE CRY OUT FOR THOSE WITH NO VOICE?

The need for justice is not confined to the sex trade. The prophetic outcry for justice covers the whole world.

One wintry day in February 2006, I was standing before the Supreme Court in Washington, D.C. with Lou Engle and his team from the Justice House of Prayer. We were prophesying—but we were not saying a word. Or were we?

As we stood there in a lineup with over 80 others on that particular day (as Lou's team did every day), each of us had a strip of red adhesive tape taped across our mouths. We stood there in stark silence, portraying visually the cry of unborn children who cannot defend themselves from being killed by abortion. The cry of an unborn baby is inaudible and it cannot be heard with our ears. So others have to cry out for their protection. Someone has to represent their small but desperate voices, trumpeting the cause of justice and life.

Our effort was a small part of a much larger one. Through massive prophetic calls to prayer, solemn assemblies, and repentance, media exposure grew. The prophetic love message of justice for the unborn broke through ignorance and resistance, spreading like wildfire. Believers all across the United States began to cry out before God for these yet-unborn children. Silent but articulate, their prophetic voice began to be noticed by politicians and representatives of the justice system. Best of all, however, was the fact that many women who had planned to have abortions changed their minds. The prophetic trumpet of justice had sounded clearly.

Once again, the voice of God had become audible to ears and hearts that had never before heard Him speak. In the war against wickedness, a beachhead of justice had been established without the firing of a single shot—or the speaking of a single perceptible prophetic word.

IN THE CENTER OF GOD'S WILL

At one time, I lived a safe and predictable existence in a middle-class neighborhood. I still live a safe existence—because of angelic protection—and yet it is far from predictable.

I never knew that such devastation and depravity existed in the cities of North America and across the world. If someone had told me that I would someday be "street smart" in the way that I am now, I would have thought they were talking about someone else. Day after day and year after year, I am carried forward by the prophetic message that I express (and that I also train others to express) to the lost people who have no one else to tell them about God's loving justice.

My heart goes out the most to the women and children who have been exploited and abandoned by others who are more corrupt and wicked than seems possible. And yet, when the Spirit pulls back the veil to reveal the lostness of the perpetrators of unrighteousness, my heart goes out to them as well. God's indiscriminating love can penetrate the darkest of hearts in a moment of time.

All of them, abusers and abused, live in an atmosphere that is permeated with the stench of death. Most of them have experienced death first-hand in the neglected inner cores of cities where violence, crime, suicide, and a rampant drug culture punctuate every day with gunshots, screams, sirens, and alarms. Children, locked into apartments and seedy rooms for their own protection, cannot use the derelict playgrounds anyway, littered as they are with discarded hypodermic needles and trash. It takes your breath away.

Where is the breath of God in such places? For the rest of my earthly existence, I will cry out with a prophetic voice for God's righteousness and justice to prevail in the darkness. In the words of the psalmist:

> *Righteous are You, O Lord, and upright are Your judgments.*
> *Your testimonies, which You have commanded, are righteous*

and very faithful. My zeal has consumed me, because my enemies have forgotten Your words. Your word is very pure; therefore Your servant loves it. I am small and despised, yet I do not forget Your precepts. Your righteousness is an everlasting righteousness, and Your law is truth…The righteousness of Your testimonies is everlasting; give me understanding, and I shall live. I cry out with my whole heart; hear me, O Lord!…I cry out to You; save me, and I will keep Your testimonies. I rise before the dawning of the morning, and cry for help; I hope in Your word. My eyes are awake through the night watches, that I may meditate on Your word. Hear my voice according to Your lovingkindness; O Lord, revive me according to Your justice. They draw near who follow after wickedness; they are far from Your law. You are near, O Lord, and all Your commandments are truth. Concerning Your testimonies, I have known of old that You have founded them forever (Psalm 119:137-142,144-152).

Chapter 6

The Prophetic
and the Realm of Glory
Jeff Jansen

For the past few years, we have been hearing a lot about "the glory realm." People have been having supernatural encounters with angels as well as some very unique manifestations of power and blessing.

Prior to this wave of glory, people in the Church were talking more about the prophetic. It is not as if we have now forgotten about the prophetic, nor have we forgotten about healing or evangelism or any of the other incredible moves of the Holy Spirit that have captured our attention over the years. Each special emphasis is one more taste of Heaven, and they are all interrelated and connected.

What Is the Realm of Glory?

Our heritage as the King's sons and daughters includes being able to function in the realm of "glory." What do I mean by that? Can "the realm of glory" be defined?

In order to describe the glory realm, which is the realm of the Spirit, it is necessary first to understand something about how it correlates with the natural realm. Here is how it works. The physical world was created from the Spirit realm. Everything that we can see, touch, smell, hear, and taste has been birthed from a realm that we cannot detect with our five natural senses. The Word, Jesus, who has existed eternally, created it by speaking it into existence. (See Genesis 1 and John 1.)

Scripture says that the natural person cannot perceive spiritual things:

> The natural man does not receive the things of the Spirit of God, for they are foolishness to him; nor can he know them, because they are spiritually discerned (1 Corinthians 2:14).

In other words, we can discern spiritual things only with our spirits; our "spirit man" receives revelation from the realm of the Spirit. Between these two realms, the natural and the spiritual, supernatural substance flows back and forth.

Paul prayed that you might be sanctified—spirit, soul, and body (see 1 Thess. 5:23). Notice the order—spirit-soul-body, not body, soul, and spirit as we usually list them. The spirit comes first because the Spirit creates first the human spirit, then the soul, and then the body. If you pat yourself on the arm right now, you are not touching the real you; you are touching only your outer self, your flesh. The real you is a spirit. Your spirit lives in a body, which gets you around while you are on earth almost the same way your car takes you where you want to drive.

You are an eternal individual, an eternal spirit. You existed in the very mind of God before you existed in your body of flesh. You came from Him. You are His seed. He is your Daddy. He knows you and you know Him. God spoke to Job and said, *"Brace yourself like a man; I will question you, and you shall answer me. 'Where were you when I laid the earth's foundation? Tell me, if you understand'"* (Job 38:3-4 NIV). We usually read that as if God was challenging Job, but He was really getting Job to think about reality. He was trying to jog his memory. He was saying, "Come on, Job, you know this. You are a spirit person. I want you to remember. You know you are not here by chance."

The real you is a spirit. You need to be very clear on this fact. When the devil tries to tell you that you are less than a spirit, just a mere human being, he is putting you down so that he can take advantage of you.

Releasing the Realm of Glory

Most of us have a hard time thinking beyond what we can see, touch, smell, hear, and taste, and our problems weigh us down. God needs to remind each one of us that He created us and placed us here, that He has a plan for our lives, that we have resources beyond our earthly supply, and that we have the full imprint of the measure of God in our spirits. With our spirits, we connect with Him and with all that He wants to do for us and through us.

Some people are more sensitive to the spirit realm than others. But anyone can learn to be more sensitive with practice because everyone has a spirit. Everyone's spirit can receive revelation from the spirit realm. The main reason we do not see more of the supernatural flow manifesting from Heaven is because we have not discerned what God is releasing.

The other reason we do not see more of the supernatural flow is because we have not done anything with what we may have discerned. When we can see something in the spirit realm *and* we can speak it into existence in the natural realm, that is when we will see miracles. When we can frame the unseen with our words, then it can become obvious to our physical senses.

That is what is going on when people receive words of knowledge. The realm of glory presses in on them and they know something in their spirits. Then, when they speak it out, it becomes established in the current time and place. Just as our Creator could speak and create the world, so He still speaks through us to re-create and restore.

In a way, it is like radio waves. Just because there are radio waves traveling through the atmosphere does not guarantee that something is going to happen. The radio waves cannot "manifest" until someone turns on a radio and tunes in to the right frequency so that the invisible radio waves resolve themselves into words and sentences. The person who tunes in can pull that dimension into the room or car where they are standing or sitting. Now they can do something with the information they receive through the radio.

Another word for this spiritual tuning-in is *faith*. Faith is "the substance of things hoped for, the evidence of things not seen" (Heb. 11:1). Faith makes unseen things discernible to our natural senses, and a word spoken in faith releases power from the glory realm, where the angels are always ready to make spiritual substance manifest in the physical realm. (Miracles, healings, signs, wonders, words of knowledge, revelation, supernatural power—the angels are the messengers of all these and more from the unseen heavenly realm.)

DISCERNING WHAT GOD IS RELEASING

If we want to see more manifestations of the supernatural flow from Heaven, we need to start discerning what God is releasing. Our spirits need to get more sensitive to God before we can start prophetically decreeing the release of His power.

Sometimes we are just too slow. (Not only do we need training in discernment, we also need quick-response training.) The dilemma for many people is that by the time they see the realm of glory coming into a room and they start to act on it, the window of opportunity has closed and they must reopen it through thanksgiving and praise and worship.

When we worship, we create a cloud of glory that is sometimes even visible. As we praise God, the atmosphere thickens and becomes spiritually heavy. When the spiritual climate is just right, we can speak into the cloud of glory and see a release of miraculous provision. If we do not speak, nothing will happen. But if the cloud is not present, nothing will happen either. We need both.

Not long ago I was in a meeting, and my ministry video team was filming the worship. About 500 of us were in the room, singing and shouting high praises to God, and we were going to keep doing it until the glory of God came. As we kept worshiping and waiting for more, you could feel the Holy Spirit moving. And yet it was not the kind of presence that indicates a time of miracles. This was just good fellowship with the Holy Spirit.

Then I started to smell burning incense. It smelled to me like burning myrrh. I thought someone behind me on the stage had lit some myrrh or frankincense, so I turned around to look. Nobody had any incense. Then it got really strong as if it were right next to me. I looked over at the pastor and he was looking around, too. It got stronger and stronger and stronger.

Then a literal cloud began to build. People were still praising God. We captured it on video. As the cloud materialized and people were waving their hands, you could see swirls around their hands. Later we broadcasted the video on the Miracle Channel and posted it on our Web site.

THE CLOUD AND THE WORD

We need both the cloud and the spoken word. This is how the glory realm ties in with the prophetic. Even when we cannot see a literal cloud, our spirits can learn to tell when it is time to speak. Unless we speak, nothing will manifest from the spiritual dimension. (But again, unless we have the atmosphere, we can speak all day long and God's power will not be manifested.)

Just as we have learned to interpret what our five senses tell us about the natural world, we can learn what our spirit is sensing. Revelation is nothing more than the revealed mechanics of God. Revelation enables us to think and operate from the supernatural dimension.

To clear the way for revelation, we must stop questioning God. Instead of always looking for logical answers for natural problems, we need to respond with the faith that He gives us. As we do, we will ascend into higher levels of the glory of God and we will see greater manifestations of the miraculous.

We do not need to worry if we think this sounds too New-Agey. If we stick close to Jesus and to His people, we won't be deceived. After all, New-Age terminology and experience was stolen from the real Kingdom. The devil is a counterfeiter, and he imitates the real thing.

THE GLORY REALM

We cannot see what God is doing in the glory realm unless we have His anointing. His anointing opens our spiritual eyes so that we can see. People talk a lot about "the anointing" as if it is synonymous with the glory, but they are two different things.

The glory of God is an atmosphere that is heavy with splendor, and the anointing is like a cloak or a mantle that comes onto a person so that the person can perceive the glory and operate in its power. The anointing gives a person supernatural ability to be able to move in the gifts of the Spirit. Jesus said:

> The Spirit of the Lord is upon Me, because He has anointed Me to preach the gospel to the poor; He has sent Me to heal the brokenhearted, to proclaim liberty to the captives and recovery of sight to the blind, to set at liberty those who are oppressed (Luke 4:18).

As important as God's anointing is, do you see that it is not the same as the glory itself? The glory itself is much greater. The glory of God can be defined in several ways:

- The glory of God is the expressed, manifested, multifaceted attributes of the godhead.

- The glory of God is His perceptible splendor, His majesty, His creative power.

- The glory of God is His holiness, His character, His goodness.

- The glory of God is His presence and love.

- The glory of God is His power, His life, resurrection life.

The glory of God is not easy to nail down. You can define it however you want to, but it all comes down to this—the glory of God is the *Person of the Lord Jesus Christ* and is the timeless *realm* that is around the throne of God in Heaven. It exists outside of time. It has always existed; it never had a beginning and it will never have an end. Before God created the physical universe, before created time, before angels, before "realms" had a context, this atmosphere of glory existed. The glory around the throne of God is His presence. It is God Himself.

In the midst of the glory around the throne are seraphim, cherubim, and heavenly beings. Just because most of us have never been there, have never experienced such glory, and have never seen these heavenly beings around the throne does not mean that this dimension does not exist. It is not just "up there" someplace. It is another dimension, and it exists alongside the dimension we live in. The glory realm is right here, right now, because it is interconnected with the physical realm. It gives life and sustains it. It is real. It is the heart of God's Kingdom, and His heart beats in both Heaven and earth at the same time.

GOD'S WORD SPOKEN IN THE REALM OF GLORY

Now this is where we come in. We are God's sons and daughters, and He has granted to His family power and authority in their spoken word for the purpose of furthering and advancing and establishing His Kingdom on earth. The Kingdom is like a family business. As our Father's delegated authorities, we further establish our Father's Kingdom on the earth through the power and authority of the spoken word, which is a prophetic function.

When God speaks, we become impregnated with His words. As time passes, His words grow and develop, eventually causing us to give birth to a specific promise. However, when God's word is spoken in the realm of glory, we see the promise instantly. The time required for growth and maturing becomes instantaneous because that realm is timeless.

Our life experience can become quite a struggle because we so easily lose sight of God's glory. When our forefather Adam sinned, the whole human race fell into sin, and the seamless unity that had existed with God was broken. *"For all have sinned and **fall short** of the glory of God"* (Rom. 3:23). Having fallen short of His glory, our spiritual eyes have been darkened. We have been cut off from that dimension; we fall short of it. Although Adam had been created to live forever in the context of God's glory, never to grow sick or old and die, his sin cut him off from the source of life. To give us a way to get back to the glory, the Second Adam, Jesus, had to come.

Now, thanks to Jesus, we can see again. Our blinded eyes have been restored. Now, in collaboration with the realm of God's glory, we can regain the perfect health and happiness that are part of our birthright. Creative power can be released for creative miracles. Babies can be born to barren women. Financial provision can come from *that realm*. Missing fingers and toes can grow out. Hair can turn from gray to black. Healings *and miracles* can happen before our very eyes, because the glory realm is a timeless *realm* of *"all things are possible."* What would normally take years to happen, if at all, can happen in a fraction of the time. A creative miracle is not just something broken or sick being fixed, healed, or revived; it is something new being created. In the presence of the glory of God, we have seen many miracles like that.

UNLOCKING THE REALM OF GLORY

Besides having the cloud of glory and the spoken word, we need several other keys to unlock the realm of glory. I have already mentioned faith. Faith is the currency that draws on the realm of glory.

Without faith, we cannot hear what God is saying. Faith operates from a higher law than the natural laws of matter, space, and time. A person of faith believes and speaks from the eternal realm of the "now," releasing the unseen realm of glory into the natural world.

Along with faith, we need vision and imagination. God gave us our imaginations, and we need to learn how to use them. If He tells us something and we can see it with our imagination, we can bring it forward into the atmosphere, declare it, and it will be made manifest for all to see. Our imaginations represent the creative side of God. He imagined everything before He spoke it into being. He thought about it first; everything He created lived in His imagination, including you and me:

> *Your eyes have seen my unformed substance; and in Your book were all written the days that were ordained for me, when as yet there was not one of them* (Psalm 139:16 NASB).

To see into the realm of the supernatural, we must be able to envision, imagine, and perceive, through faith, the things that are coming from the realm of glory. We need to become intimately acquainted with His ways, so we can know what He wants to do and then visualize it.

The glory realm is the source of all life. Jesus said, *"I am the Way and the Truth and the Life"* (John 14:6 AMP). When *Martha's* brother Lazarus died, He told *her,* *"I am the resurrection and the life"* (John 11:25). She thought He meant that her brother would rise again at the last day, but Jesus meant that His *name* was Way and Truth and Life and also Resurrection with a capital R. "Do you understand this, Martha? You are talking to the Creator. I *am* Life." When He wept, I don't think it was only from sympathy for their grief (see John 11:35). *But rather because of their unbelief,* He wept because *they did not recognize Him.*

Just before He spoke to Lazarus' dead body to tell it to come forth alive from the tomb, Jesus said to Martha, "Did I not say to you that if you would believe you would see the glory of God?" (John 11:40). And then He spoke words of life, and the dead man was restored. The Spirit of Creation, in one authoritative spoken word, brought life into that sealed tomb. This is the eternal formula for creation from Genesis to the present.

They go together—the brooding Holy Spirit, the Spirit of Creation, the atmosphere of glory that accompanies the presence of God, and the spoken word. "Let there be light," and *bam!*—manifested light was everywhere. Remember Ezekiel and the dry bones—the Holy Spirit told Ezekiel to prophesy to the bones. Ezekiel perceived what God wanted to do. He spoke authoritatively *by the Holy Spirit* and those dry bones became an army (see Ezek. 37).

In the very beginning, God gave authority to the men and women He created to populate the earth (see Gen. 1:26-28). Jesus Christ reasserted that dominion, and God has not rescinded it:

> *What is man that You are mindful of him, and the son of man that You visit him? For You have made him a little lower than the angels, and You have crowned him with glory and honor. You have made him to have dominion over the works of Your hands; You have put all things under his feet* (Psalm 8:4-6).

Someone who knows God can see what He is doing in the glory realm, and that person can bring it to earth by speaking out with his or her authority as a son or daughter of God. By faith, such a person reaches into the unseen heavenly realm so that new things can be manifested in the natural realm. Faith, perceiving as real fact what has not been revealed to the senses, is the substance and the evidence of things that are hidden in the glory realm (see Heb. 11:1). In my imagination, I can see it. I see it happening now. So I speak it. My faith frames things in real time, in "now time."

"By faith we understand that the worlds were framed by the word of God, so that the things which are seen were not made of things which are visible" (Heb. 11:3). Both the visible world and the unseen world are equipped at God's command for their intended purposes. As God continues to redeem the visible world for His Kingdom, we can participate with Him, speaking prophetically as the Spirit gives us utterance.

NEW THINGS KEPT IN RESERVE

Through the prophet Isaiah, God explains how the prophetic word—spoken about something that a person has glimpsed with his or her spirit and has laid hold of by faith—can release new things. The Lord God said:

> *I have declared the former things from the beginning; they went forth from My mouth, and I caused them to hear it. Suddenly I did them, and they came to pass* (Isaiah 48:3).

God declares what is going to happen, He causes His servants to hear and understand, and He demonstrates His sovereign power. Then those who see what He is doing can bear witness to it, and with their words they can frame the hidden things so that they will appear out of the timeless realm of God's glory:

> *You have heard; see all this. And will you not declare it? I have made you hear new things from this time, even hidden things, and you did not know them. They are created now and not from the beginning; and before this day you have not heard them...* (Isaiah 48:6-7).

As the word goes out, these new things are being drawn from the unseen glory into specific places at specific times. By seeing what God is doing and releasing it through the prophetic word, men and women are collaborating with Him. They are speaking out and calling into being things that were hidden to their natural senses. New things are being created that were unknown up to now.

Like Abraham, prophetic people believe God because God speaks to them. God spoke to Abraham about his future. He and his wife had no children and they were nomads, and yet God was predicting that his descendants would be as numerous and countless as the grains of dust on the face of the earth and that they would possess the land He was showing him (see Gen. 13:14-17). By absolute faith, Abraham framed his future by his obedient words and actions.

Having received a prophetic revelation, he could see with the spiritual eyes of his imagination and he could act. In and of themselves, his subsequent words and actions could not have called into being the events and blessings that came to pass. God's promises were fulfilled because Abraham saw them and called them into the present. He is a towering example of the kind of active faith that bridges the gap between the unseen realm and the physical one.

> *For if Abraham was justified by works, he has something to boast about, but not before God. For what does the Scripture say? "Abraham believed God, and it was accounted to him for righteousness"* (Romans 4:2-3).

He paid attention to God and he followed through.

SETTING YOUR ATTENTION ON THINGS ABOVE

If you listen, you will hear. But you need to be careful what you are listening to. If your thoughts and your attention are always focused on things around you here on earth, that is all you will know about. It might be truth. It might be reality. But the degree of revelation and power that will come back to you will be limited to what you can discern with your five senses.

> *If then you were raised with Christ, seek those things which are above, where Christ is, sitting at the right hand of God. Set your mind on things above, not on things on the earth* (Colossians 3:1-2).

The things that are above, in the glory realm, will always prevail over the things that are below in the physical realm. The things that we perceive as reality because we can touch them are less real than the heavenly reality, which is pure Truth.

During Jesus' ministry, one of the rulers of the synagogue grasped this clearly. His name was Jairus, and we find his story in Mark 5, Luke 8, and Matthew 9. As a synagogue official, I am sure that Jairus had heard many negative reports about this man named Jesus. His colleagues considered Jesus to be a dangerous deceiver, and they thought that those who associated with Him were gullible, at the least, and quite possibly criminals.

But Jairus' young daughter lay dying. He was desperate. Along with the criticisms, he had also heard accounts of the healing power of this man Jesus. Because of his great need, he chucked all of the disapproving hearsay. He found Jesus, and prostrated himself before Him. He asked for help, in faith that Jesus could do what physicians could not: *"My little daughter lies at the point of death. Come and lay Your hands on her, that she may be healed, and she will live"* (Mark 5:23).

His faith was tested further as the crowd that pressed around Jesus slowed Him down. Besides that, a woman in the crowd got healed—one who had had a long-term hemorrhaging problem—and Jesus took time to speak to her personally and to commend her for her faith (see Mark 5:25-34).

In the meantime, Jairus' daughter died! Someone came to tell him. But this did not deter Jesus. The girl's father had asked Him for help, and He intended to give it regardless of the impossible-seeming circumstances. Jesus heard the facts with His own ears. The man who came from Jairus' house had stated, *"Your daughter is dead. Why trouble the Teacher any further?"* (Mark 5:35). But *"as soon as Jesus heard the word that was spoken, He said to the ruler of the synagogue, 'Do not be afraid; only believe'"* (Mark 5:36). Jairus believed.

Remember, Jesus is the Truth, and the Truth wins out over facts every time. Jesus chose to override the physical fact of death just as He overruled the physical fact of illness. They proceeded to Jairus' house, where everything was in an uproar of grieving. When he made a statement about how their despair was uncalled-for because the girl was only sleeping, they laughed at Him. What did He know? He hadn't even been there. Her mother had seen her draw her last breath. There lay her pale body, cold and clammy and lifeless.

But the One who was also called the Life, taking with him only those whose faith was sufficient, strode up to the girl's deathbed. He picked up her limp hand. The Spirit of Life spoke to her departed spirit and released resurrection:

> He...said to her, "Talitha, cumi," which is translated, "Little girl, I say to you, arise." Immediately the girl arose and walked, for she was twelve years of age. And they were overcome with great amazement (Mark 5:41-42).

Jesus called life back into the girl the same way that we can learn to call life into any situation. Having set His mind on things that are above, He was positioned to grasp the Truth—what the Father wanted to do right that minute—and He could speak it into being. He is our model of how it can be done, and He has paid the price so that we can do it too.

God does not run everything past us for approval; He is sovereign. But He will reveal His intentions to those who belong to Him and who seek Him out. In His presence, putting faith in His goodness as well as in His desire to do a particular thing, we can open our mouths and decree life—healing, miracles, signs, and wonders. And we will see results.

RAISING UP AN APOSTOLIC GENERATION

Just as Jesus raised a 12-year-old girl, so He is raising a generation that is mantled with apostolic governing power. Twelve is the number of government and of the apostolic.[1] I believe that apostolic government is coming into view. At present, we can point to some models out there and they are headed in the right direction, but what we will start to see is apostolic government backed up with the Kingdom of power *and glory*.

This apostolic generation will demonstrate signs and wonders *and* release the government of God throughout the earth. Increasingly through this generation, the Kingdom will come on earth as it is in Heaven (see Matt. 6:10). *This* apostolic generation is the family of God, sons and daughters who understand their *position, place,* and *identity.* They owe their birthright not to a geographical or socioeconomic place but to another dimension, the one called the Kingdom of God. They have been born from above, "not of blood, nor of the will of the flesh, nor of the will of man, but of God" (John 1:13).

These sons and daughters understand that their citizenship is from Heaven. They understand that their elder brother Jesus has earned them joint seating with God. They comprehend that they are dual-dimensional individuals who dwell on the earth and simultaneously in the heavenly dimension.

Everywhere they go, this apostolic generation releases the government of God. If you do not want to call it "apostolic" (applying the word broadly), simply call it "family." These sons and daughters are stepping into the place that God originally designated for His sons and daughters, a place from which they can take dominion as they implement God's will and His government on the earth.

Jairus experienced apostolic government. He experienced Jesus standing in His place as the Son of God and the Son of Man, speaking with heavenly authority. Jesus was filled with the Holy Spirit. God was living on the inside of Him and moving on the outside. He was a prototype of a brand new kind of human being who would help implement the will of God. He released the will of God by speaking the word of God.

Carrying the cloud of glory with Him, He spoke and resurrection power was released into Jairus' 12-year-old daughter. In the same way, He spoke and His friend Lazarus rose from the dead. And in the same way, the members of the new apostolic generation, operating under God's anointing, speak prophetically and introduce the Kingdom realm wherever they go. This is *"Christ in you, the hope of glory"* (Col. 1:27).

CHRIST IN YOU, THE HOPE OF GLORY

With the timelessness of Heaven flowing through our words, we find ourselves in a place of compounded time. The plowman will soon overtake the reaper (see Amos 9:13). Time is running into eternity.

This is why we are seeing so much more evidence of glory—more angelic encounters, heavenly visitations, and unexplainable signs such as deposits of gold, feathers, and beautiful gemstones. It seems crazy sometimes, but we know that such signs only point the way to their source.

I got a call from a pastor in Idaho telling me how a number of prophetic words from reputable people were fulfilled. Among the many signs that had occurred was the one when an usher (whose last name happened to be Copper) got covered with *gold* during the offertory prayer. They opened their eyes after the prayer and there he was, covered with gold. It was running out of his ears, eyes, and nose. He opened his mouth and everything inside was gold. The offering bucket he was holding was gold. Gold was pouring down on him and he was weeping with amazement because up to then he had not even believed in supernatural signs. On top of that, his eyes were opened to the glory realm and he started to see angels.

Shortly after that, big gemstones began to appear out of nowhere, 40 in all. The same thing began to happen in other churches. All of this has been hard to explain, although people are trying. The prophet Bob Jones says they are the "glistening stones" that Solomon gathered for the house of God, which represent the spiritual house of God (see 1 Chron. 29:2).

The Spirit of God is doing unusual things, and the dimension from which these artifacts come is the same dimension from which healing and miracles come. It is the glory dimension in which eyes replace empty sockets and diseased hearts are recreated with healthy muscle. From this same dimension, you receive from the Holy Spirit a "now" word that proceeds to manifest while you are still speaking.

To help us understand, God has been leading us to Scripture such as this:

Does not wisdom cry out, and understanding lift up her voice? She takes her stand on the top of the high hill, beside the way, where the paths meet. She cries out by the gates, at the entry of the city, at the entrance of the doors: "To you, O men, I call, and my voice is to the sons of men" (Proverbs 8:1-4).

At the entry doors of the town, Wisdom (personified as a woman) cries out. Here we see "paths" and "gates" and "the entrance of the doors," just as in the Book of Jeremiah we see "ancient paths" (see Jer. 18:15). There really are supernatural ways, supernatural portals, and that is how the angels move. It is not as mystical as you may think. After all, Jesus said He was a Door and His sheep would be able to hear His voice so that they could go in and out and find rest for their souls (see John 10:1-16).

Go in and out of where? In and out of the realm of the Spirit, the glory realm. You can try to go in and out of the back door, but you cannot do it. You can get good information together, even spiritual information, but if you did not enter through the Door named Jesus, you will have gotten it from demons.

The glory realm is the Real. When you encounter that realm, things open up and you can see miracles whether your eyes are closed or open because you are functioning in two dimensions at the same time. They are interacting.

We Are Connectors

You and I are the connectors between these realms. We hold the keys. The keys come from the Spirit, and He teaches us how to use them.

As we spend time with the Lord, approaching His throne in worship, setting our minds on things above, and praying in the Spirit, we will grow in our ability to perceive what He wants us to do. To hear Him, we will not have to stay in our prayer closets all the time. On the street, in the car, in the mall, we will serve God's purposes by partnering with *the angelic realm.*

We are supernatural connectors because we have been *born from above.* We were created as flesh and blood in the natural realm and our spirits have *encountered a rebirthing* from above. We can move with our elder brother Jesus as He shows us the way. We are His voice on the earth. As we open our mouths and speak prophetic words, the realm of glory will be made manifest right here and now.

ENDNOTE

1. For example, in the Bible we see twelve apostles as well as 12 tribes of Israel. The heavenly city of Jerusalem has twelve foundations: 12 gates, 12 pearls, and 12 angels and it measures 12,000 stadia.

Chapter 7

PROPHETIC INTERCESSION
Michal Ann Goll

Although Michal Ann went home to the Lord in September of 2008, I have included a chapter based on some of her excellent unpublished teachings on the topic of prophetic intercession, about which she was so very passionate.

—James W. Goll

I have spent a lot of time in prayer meetings over the years. In some of them, the atmosphere has been charged with the presence of God and the prayers were dynamic. After others, I would walk out wondering, "What did we just do anyway? Did it make any difference?"

If you have been a Christian for very long, you know what I am describing. You walk into the room for the prayer meeting and everybody sits down. Someone says, "Let's pray." Then an invisible pressure begins to build: "We've got to pray. We've got to pray…." People feel they are supposed to pray out loud and that long silences are to be avoided, so before waiting to hear what the Lord is saying, someone starts off praying. Then another person prays, and another, praying whatever they can think of. A lot of prayer activity may occur, but the meeting is what my husband James calls "popcorn prayer"—pop here, pop there, with no continuity. Individuals are verbalizing prayers they think they should pray, often in biblical language, but they are not laying down their own agendas long enough to listen and find out what God's agenda is.

Prophetic intercession is different. It is an adventure! Prophetic intercession is not even the same as bringing your personal prayer requests to God. Prophetic intercession flips the equation—God brings His requests to *you*, and you intercede on behalf of the people, places, and actions that He has on His heart. This kind of praying is prophetic because you cannot do it at all unless you first hear the voice of God. You are speaking His words and ideas back to Him.

The Lord shows us things in pictures and in simple terminology because He wants us to understand Him. For example, He helped the prophet Isaiah paint a word picture of an intercessor:

> *On your walls, O Jerusalem, I have appointed watchmen; all day and all night they will never keep silent you who remind the Lord, take no rest for yourselves; and give Him no rest until He establishes and makes Jerusalem a praise in the earth* (Isaiah 62:6-7 NASB).

The Lord has appointed each of us as watchmen over a portion of His Kingdom. He has called us for the purpose of helping to establish that Kingdom across the face of the earth. Prophetic intercession/watching is both a responsibility and a privilege, and it must be born out of a faithful love relationship with the King. He tells His watchmen where to stand and what to do, and they report back to Him.

While it is true that Jesus established the Church (and called it His Bride) out of His love, He does not want His people to be Church-oriented. Rather, He wants His people to be Kingdom-oriented, helping to bring His Kingdom to earth. That was His mission when he ministered as a man (see Luke 4:43; 8:1; Matt. 4:23; 9:35). He has commissioned us to continue doing it (see Matt. 24:4; Luke 9:2,60). Prophetic intercession is all-important to the establishment of the Kingdom of God on earth.

WHAT IS A PROPHETIC INTERCESSOR?

So what does a prophetic intercessor do? In order to better define a prophetic intercessor, first we must review what an intercessor or watchman is. I will refer to some of the definitions that my husband, James Goll, included in his book, *The Prophetic Intercessor,* and the study guide, *Compassionate Prophetic Intercession.*

- An intercessor is one who reminds the Lord of promises and appointments yet to be met and fulfilled. An intercessor reads the Bible with close attention to God's promises. An intercessor knows that God loves to hear prayers that are based on those promises.

- An intercessor takes up a case of justice before God on behalf of another. Unless someone intercedes, God cannot make right the injustices that afflict a person or a group of people (see Isa. 59:15-16).

- In a time of battle, an intercessor is one who helps to build the wall for defensive as well as offensive purposes. God admonished the prophet-intercessors of Israel for *not* doing this: "O Israel, your prophets are like foxes in the deserts. You have not gone up into the gaps to build a wall ["hedge" in the King James version] for the house of Israel to stand in battle on the day of the Lord" (Ezek. 13:4-5).

- On the people's behalf, an intercessor stands in the gap between God's righteous judgment and the need for mercy. *"So I sought for a man among them who would make a wall, and stand in the gap before Me on behalf of the land, that I should not destroy it; but I found no one"* (Ezek. 22:30). God is always searching for more intercessors, people whose hearts are aligned with His and who are willing to spend time on their knees on behalf of others.

In a limited way, any person of prayer can perform these functions on his or her own initiative. Convinced that it is the right thing to do, any believer can take on a cause in prayer. Prayer groups have done this for years. It is not wasted effort, although the strength to carry on will dwindle over time.

So many of the things that we need to pray for are daunting. They are too big for us and we know it. How much better it is to pray in a more focused way, with renewed energy daily, receiving and praying with prophetic words (as recorded in the Bible or as recorded on the tablets of our human hearts).

Here are two working definitions of prophetic intercession:

- Prophetic intercession is the ability to receive an immediate prayer request from God and pray about it in a divinely anointed utterance.

- Prophetic intercession is waiting before God in order to hear or sense His will or receive His burden (His word, His concerns, His warnings, His conditions, His vision, or His promises), then responding back to Him with appropriate prayers and actions.

A prophetic intercessor is someone who can hear the voice of God and who then prays according to what He says. Prophetic intercession happens when the spirit of prophecy and the desire to intercede are mingled in one person or group. Not everyone is called to the office of prophet, but all of us are enjoined to seek the gift of prophecy (see 1 Cor. 14:1). One of the most important applications of that gift is in the realm of prayer.

ORCHESTRATION

Intercessory prayer must flow like a symphony, with every member of the "prayer orchestra" tuned together and playing the same piece of music. There's no way in the world that an orchestra is going to be able to play a melody if each musician follows his or her own ideas, picks out different songs, plays at different rhythms, and tunes to different pitches. I used to play the flute in high school and I could practice at home, thinking my instrument was tuned well, only to go to practice at school and find out that it was not.

One good reason to pray with other people is to find out if you are "in tune" with God's heart or not. You do not have to be praying with a large group of people, but you do need some others to tune up with. You cannot stay in tune all by yourself. Praying with other people will also help you learn when to refrain from speaking and when to speak up. Together you can be a little orchestra of intercession, each of you focusing on the tip of the Conductor's baton. You are ready to play (pray) with your music out. Along with the others, you are watching the tip of that baton, and you do not do anything until that baton moves. Then you follow the direction of the Conductor and the music He wants you to play. Not only do you play only the notes that have been assigned to your instrument, you also learn to pay attention to instructions about crescendos and decrescendos and silent rests.

This is not the time to pull out your prayer list. It is time to lay all of your own agendas down in favor of one agenda—His. When you come into a corporate prayer setting, it is time to walk away from your identity and to become part of a corporate entity. You are linked together; together you pray as one voice, like an orchestra.

You need to be strong in your sense of identity as a son or daughter of God in order to lay down your personal agenda like that. I learned this early in my marriage. I had grown up as a country girl, and I spent a lot of time alone because we lived fifteen miles from the nearest town and the closest girl (who was not a particularly close friend) lived on a farm half a mile away. As a result, I spent a lot of time reading my Bible and going out into the pastures to pray, and I got to know my Shepherd's voice.

Then I met and married my husband, who was miles ahead of me (and everyone else in our college group) in prophetic gifting. James was prophesying over anything and everything that moved. I didn't feel I could hear the Lord the way he could and I began to equate gifting with someone's quality of relationship with God. Consequently, when we would be at prayer and worship meetings and I would receive a song from the Lord, rather than launching out and singing the song, I would elbow Jim and say, "Hey, I think I have a song of the Lord; what do you think?" He never once said no. He would always say, "Yeah, do it!" So I would sing the song.

After a few months of doing that, I was getting ready to nudge him one more time, and the Holy Spirit stopped me and He said, "Is he your God or am I?" I was convicted. I had been leaning on my husband in the wrong way. Instead of listening to the Lord and being obedient to Him, I was always double-checking everything with Jim. After the Lord said that, I discovered something else—my spiritual hearing had become faint. It took me awhile to learn to hear God's voice again. I had to go through a season of fine-tuning the hearing of my spirit.

By the way, if you want to improve your hearing ability, use the gift of tongues. The Bible tells us that *"One who speaks in a tongue edifies himself; but one who prophesies edifies the church"* (1 Cor. 14:4 NASB). When you pray in tongues, you are putting out your spiritual antenna, which in turn helps you to receive more from God.

THE SIMPLER, THE BETTER

Give it to me simple. This is really the crux of the issue. All of us can think of all kinds of things to pray for. But when we learn to hear the voice of the Father so that we can know what He wants us to pray for, it is a lot simpler.

Simpler, but maybe not faster. I have been part of prayer gatherings in which we all sat and waited in silence for thirty or forty minutes straight. We knew that God is not anxious for anything and that it does not bother Him to have times of quietness. In fact, sometimes He uses those times to draw the insecurities out of us. Little things start to poke into our consciousness and our spirits get more agitated than we would like them to be. Somebody may think, *Maybe now's the time for a song.* Maybe. But maybe not. Maybe instead it is time to press through a little discomfort into a new level of intimacy with the Lord.

When you are learning to pray this way, you will have to be realistic. Prophetic intercession, especially with a group, is not a routine thing for most of us, and we need to grow into it. We need to be patient with ourselves and with each other, because it is not going to be perfect. We will still pray popcorn prayers and miss cues from the Holy Spirit. We will need to dialogue about what we are doing, saying things like, "Did you feel anything? Here is what I was getting earlier," and so on.

If you have someone in the group who is an accomplished prophet, the rest of the group will need to learn to be humbly honest about their comprehension level. I have been in meetings over the years with Bob Jones, who speaks in very symbolic prophetic language, and often he will say, "Do you understand what I mean?" Everybody in the room will say, "Oh yeah, yeah," until Bob steps out of the room for a minute. Then people turn to each other and whisper, "What did he say; what did he mean?"

We've got it backward. When something like that happens, just say, "I don't understand," and ask for clarification. You may comprehend 70 percent of the vision or word, but if you ask the prophet to become an interpreter, you might end up getting a whole lot more out of it. I cannot tell you how many gems of prayer wisdom I have gotten just because I dared to say, "I don't get it." It is OK to be honest and real; when you come into a prayer meeting, you do not have to turn yourself into somebody who is super-spiritual.

Being in a learning and growing process together helps us learn how we are supposed to function in the group. We discover each other's gifts, strengths, and weaknesses and we learn whom we can lean on. Over time, as we gain experience in praying together, we know who will be best able to come into a meeting having prepared his or her heart, having dealt with all the "stuff" and having wiped the slate clean in order to be ready to engage with God's Spirit.

We begin to get a corporate identity. We pull together better. We become more like a family. The journey is worth it.

Better Caught than Taught

I am trying to teach about it, but really prophetic intercession is better caught than taught. There is no substitute for being in the presence of the Lord. There is nothing like feeling a burden from God come over every member of a group in a corporate way and then pulling together to carry that burden in prayer and release it back to the Lord. Nothing compares to the actual experience of prophetic prayer.

One year in our annual Women on the Frontlines Conference, the Holy Spirit rearranged the entire afternoon into a prayer meeting of about 700 women. In that meeting, somebody mentioned that the man who had developed the partial birth abortion technique came from that geographical area. We decided to pray about that. Many of us felt that the spirit that allowed him to develop that technique was in direct opposition to the purposes of God's Spirit for the region, which had to do with evangelism and Kingdom reproduction.

Before we could pray effectively, we had to seek out the root of that anti-life spirit. The Holy Spirit just landed on us as a group. By the grace of God, as we made ourselves available to Him to carry whatever He wanted us to carry, we began to cry out, standing in the gap for that region. We prayed as though we were the ones who had come up with that medical technique and we cried out to the Lord for forgiveness. We understood that when you come together for prophetic intercession, it is no longer "us" versus "them." It's all "us." We had to take on that sin as though we had done it ourselves. With many tears, we took it on and we asked the Lord to forgive us.

After working through those prayers for a while, we decided to apply our prayers to a practical application. So we called forward any women who were barren and unable to have children; after all, the Lord had healed me of that condition and enabled me to have four miracle children. We prayed for healing power and we took every opportunity to help them step into their destiny as they represented the whole region. We prayed all afternoon.

Then, quite suddenly, that heavy burden was gone. How can that happen? How can you be carrying a burden one minute and the next minute—poof!—it's gone? The Holy Spirit does that all the time, and you have to experience it to know what it feels like. Some of the burden-bearing seasons will be a few moments long. Other times, you will carry a burden nine months, as though you were carrying a child to birth, or longer. You carry the burden until the Holy Spirit releases you from it. That is a big part of prophetic intercession, and you need to be aware of it before you volunteer for duty.

VOLUNTEER FOR DUTY

If you are not a prophetic intercessor already, what does it mean for you to become one? The Lord wants us all to volunteer, although He does not fill in all the blanks ahead of time. It is an adventure! Don't you want to venture out into the unknown?

Volunteering for duty takes you into the heart of God, and once you get into His heart, you get drawn in farther and farther. You can't tell where you are going and you would not be able to imagine it if He told you ahead of time. You will never know what God is going to have you do and what He will birth through you. Our prophetic prayer is a birthing ground. All of our other efforts in the Kingdom need to be based on it.

When you volunteer for duty, you start by laying down your personal agenda. You embark on a journey of love with your heavenly Father and you assent to the idea that you will not be in the driver's seat.

He Makes It Personal

When you become a prophetic intercessor, you lay down personal goals and aspirations in favor of a personal, relational journey with your Lord. Like many things in the Kingdom, it is paradoxical.

Years ago, I had a dream in which my husband and I were entering a coliseum along with thousands of other people. I knew we were going to "view the king's proceedings." As each woman entered she was given a number, but the men were not given a number. When I walked through the turnstile, James and I got separated and I did not see him for the rest of the dream. I was assigned the number 29.

I went on in and found a seat and I tried to be friendly to the lady who was sitting next to me. For some reason, even though I had not had time to do anything, she found me irritating. I was determined to make her like me, so I went to get her a glass of water. All that did was to make her all the more infuriated. She was smoking a cigarette and she sprinkled her ashes on top of my head. I was thinking, *OK, I came here to view the king's proceedings and I am sitting by this woman who is sprinkling cigarette ashes on my head. What's going on?* (You know dreams are mysteries and they often raise more questions than they answer!)

Prior to the "king's proceedings," the officials were getting ready to call women's numbers. We were told that if your number was called, that meant you had to go spend the night with whatever man they chose. This woman sitting beside me was so irritated at me that she was doing anything she could to embarrass me. So as they asked for a number, she called out mine—"Twenty-nine!" I jumped over the back of my chair and ran out of the coliseum because I did not want to go forward.

What I didn't know and what nobody knew was that the king's son was standing behind a curtain and he was going to pick his bride that day. And when he saw me run, he put his finger to his mouth and said, "Oh, I choose *her!*" So now everybody was buzzing, "Where did she go?" Nobody could find me.

All of a sudden, I re-entered the coliseum. I knew it was me, but my face looked different, and I was dressed in regal robes. I went down the steps to the floor of the coliseum and the king's son kissed me, handed me a scepter, and escorted me to the throne chair next to his. That is where the dream ended.

When I woke up, I realized that my dream was not about me. It was about all of us. This is like the invitation that the Lord gives us. For years afterward, I asked the Lord, "Why 29? What does that number have to do with anything? I don't understand." Little by little, the Lord began to unfold various "two-nine" Scriptures to me, such as the following:

> *For I know the thoughts that I think toward you, says the Lord, thoughts of peace and not of evil, to give you a future and a hope (Jeremiah 29:11).*

> *Now the young woman pleased him, and she obtained his favor; so he readily gave beauty preparations to her, besides her allowance. Then seven choice maidservants were provided for her from the king's palace, and he moved her and her maidservants to the best place in the house of the women (Esther 2:9).*

> *The voice of the Lord shakes the wilderness; the Lord shakes the Wilderness of Kadesh. The voice of the Lord makes the deer give birth, and strips the forests bare; and in His temple everyone says, "Glory!" (Psalm 29:8-9)*

> *The Lord knows how to deliver the godly out of temptations and to reserve the unjust under punishment for the day of judgment (2 Peter 2:9).*

I found even more. One day I realized that the Book of Acts has 28 chapters; it does not have a chapter 29. That is significant because it means you and I are *writing* Acts 29 ourselves.

All of the passages are about being chosen by the Lord. When He says we are chosen, He really means it. He wants to crown each one of us and to show us how His perfect love will cast out our fear and insecurity. He wants to show us (both men and women—the Church) how to be His Bride, the Bride of Christ, a warrior bride.

A pendulum swings between war and love. Sometimes we engage in tough spiritual warfare. Other times we soak in God's love and peace. As the pendulum swings, we find that the deeper our devotion, the more effective our warfare. We have to have both sides. When you and I volunteer for active duty as prophetic warriors, our effectiveness will depend on our personal love relationship with the King.

Through Pain to Authority

Part of the reason for the connection between warring and loving is the timeless truth that gets summarized as "no pain, no gain." Each one of us will find that we have the greatest authority in prayer in the areas in which we have had the most pain.

For example, James and I were barren. We could not have children. We went through years of grueling, terribly embarrassing questions and tests and crushing disappointments. Finally a specialist told us, "There are just too many things wrong here. You might as well face the fact that you are not going to have children."

Within a short time, James had a dream in which he heard a voice that said, "You are going to have a son and his name will be called Justin." When he told me about the dream, somehow it was as if I knew my son already. Still, we went through more months of disappointment.

Maybe Justin was supposed to be our adopted son? We began to consider adoption, to the point that we actually made an appointment with an agency in St. Louis. When we walked into the waiting room, I don't think I had ever been in a room with more hurting people in my life. That is when the Holy Spirit came to us and said, "Do you really think this is what I have for you?" It was as if He had said, "Can you dare to believe that I still have a son for you that is of your own body?" So we walked out. We gave our place to others in the room who needed our appointment time. We went home and began to tell people that the Lord had told us we were going to have a son. I'm sure some of them thought we were crazy.

It was like being in a desert, and it wasn't only about having children. The church we pastored was in a college town, and we would lose half our congregation every four years when the seniors would graduate and move away. We had inherited a building program we were not sure we wanted. The basement flooded three times. I had times of severe cramping, like miscarrying. We came to the end of being able to comfort each other. It was a very hard time.

One day, I told the Lord, "If you don't want me to have children, I won't like it, but I will submit myself to Your will for my life."

He responded immediately. He said, "I appreciate your attitude, but that is not what I am requiring of you. However, you are going to have to fight for your children." That statement shone a bright light into my mind and I realized that I had been blaming the Lord for my barrenness when I should have been blaming the enemy. So I shifted into high gear against the devil. After that, I was able to shift into higher gear in prayer as well because God started to show me how much *He* wanted children—even more than I did. That was the beginning of our learning about prophetic intercession.

What was on His heart? His children. Where was the dividing line between physical barrenness and spiritual barrenness? There really isn't one.

Meantime, we did premarital counseling with young couples and James performed their marriage ceremonies. It seemed as if every bride would get pregnant right away after the honeymoon, so we had endless baby dedications, too. Meanwhile, here were Jim and Ann (as we were known back then), who didn't have any children but who were sure talking about it all the time. Every time anybody wanted to pray for healing, we would get in line. We got prayed for again and again.

Finally we came to the point one night, after a long, long, meeting, the last prayer call was for women who were barren. We ran up. Mahesh Chavda was praying, and this was the third time he had prayed for us. He looked at me and said, "I see you as the joyous mother of three children." James and I just went down together under God's power, and I started to feel a warmth in my midsection that lasted for three days total. Two months later, I was pregnant.

The place of barrenness turned out to be the very place that James and I learned how to tap into the heart of God. We learned a new way of living. We learned to be in communion with Him all the time so that we can understand what the Father is doing and pray accordingly.

The very place that the enemy has attacked you and nailed you is the very place that God wants to empower you with faith and authority—it has to bring you down to the bedrock of intimacy, knowing Him, being real with Him. It gives Him something to respond to.

With each child (and I ended up being the joyous mother of four children, not only three), we had to go through extreme hardship. Each one was a new revelation of God's love. Each time, the promise was birthed through the power of travailing intercession.

CHANGING PRECONCEIVED NOTIONS

Before we had our children, a man in our church who had become a great friend wanted to prophesy over us. He wanted to speak over Jim first, so he said, "OK, Ann, I want you to go over there and sit on that bench and let me give a word to Jim first." So, with anticipation, I sat down to wait.

He started to give Jim this huge, long, incredible prophetic word. I was thinking, *Wow, Jim's word is so good. That means my word is going to be really good too.* I waited and waited.

Our friend finished prophesying and he sat down. He never called me over. I was ready, but he never called my name. All of a sudden, I realized that I had just *had* my prophetic word. My prophetic word was sitting on that bench and waiting. That was not fun at all! I felt embarrassed at the time.

The Lord had rearranged my preconceived notions. He wanted me to understand that my worth did not hinge on how long and elaborate my prophetic word was. He wanted me to understand that He knew how to talk to me perfectly in a language I could understand. He wanted me to know that the ways of God are definitely not the ways of my human flesh.

He also wanted me to know that He always works things out for the best with those who love Him—and that includes me. He showed me the same thing when He redeemed my name, Michal Ann. In the Bible, Michal is King David's first wife. She is remembered as the one who mocked her husband when he danced before the Lord (see 2 Sam. 6:16). As a result, God smote her with barrenness and she could never have a child. For some reason, my mother chose that name for me. I liked the name all right, but I did not like what the Michal in the Bible had done. I tried to be extra-careful not to judge or disdain things because I did not want to have a barren life. Little did I know that I would have to walk through years of barrenness in the first part of my married life.

For a lot of my life I just went by Ann. It was too confusing to go by Michal, especially in school where people would think I was a boy. In high school I got mailings from the Marine Corps and people would put a "Mr." in front of my name. Somewhere along the line, I began to sense that the Lord wanted me to go by my whole name. I felt He was saying, "Your whole name is a testimony of My faithfulness to you."

One day a Messianic Jewish friend offered to look up the meaning of the name Michal. As it turns out, *Michal* means "who is like God." I had never known that. I did know that *Ann* meant "grace." So it turned out that when I used my full name, I was making a statement about God's grace. Changing my preconceived notions about my name helped to bring me out of barrenness and into fruitfulness.

You can do this with any problem situation. Just flip the problem into a blessing and use prophetic tools of spiritual warfare to the glory of God!

Learning How to Contend

When He told me that I would have to fight for my children, I knew I would have to learn to contend. As I mentioned earlier, prophetic intercessors combine a warrior side with a lover side. We have to learn how to contend for the things that our Bridegroom, in His love, wants us to have.

The statement "Fight for your children" was like war orders from my Bridegroom. He had allowed me to enter His heavenly courtroom. As a righteous Judge, He was requiring me to fight. In complete dependence on Him as a just Judge, I would stand in the courtroom of Heaven declaring His words back to Him. As I contended for the births of my children, God would be making things right. He is a God of justice, and I was going to experience that firsthand.

You know, everything the enemy has ever tried to steal from you will be repaid eventually, seven times over (see Prov. 6:30-31). Every time the devil attacks you, he is just digging a deeper hole for himself because you have a righteous Judge looking out for you. Your Judge invites you to come before Him to present your petitions. You have the right to go into His heavenly courtroom and say, "OK, the thief has come and he has stolen this from me, and I call for that thief to be caught in the name of Jesus. I call for that thief to be brought into the courtroom of Heaven and for justice and recompense to be released to me."

Each one of us can do this. Each one of us is supposed to contend in that way for our own lives, and, united in a corporate way, we are supposed to contend in prayer for greater justice to be released. When we link arms with one another, we take on a corporate burden. We share the load and we pool our strength. The very things that you have walked through personally and have gained authority over you will be able to contribute to a joint prayer effort. Your faith will be greater for some things, and other people's faith will be greater in others. We need each other.

Alone or as a group, we can come into the Judge's chambers and present a case. Entering through the blood of Jesus, we can come into the throne room to bring our petition. We can call for justice to be released and we are confident that we have come to the right place to ask for it. We even dare to ask for a sevenfold recompense. We shift from being a victim to being victorious because the righteous Judge is judging on our behalf.

The enemy makes himself vulnerable the minute he rises up against someone. The Lord gave me another key to defeating the enemy in prayer and it is this. When the enemy rises up against you, he inadvertently exposes his underbelly. He's right over the top of you. So take your sword of the Spirit and push it right up into his soft belly. Contend!

PROPHETIC INTERCESSION: BIRTHING THE KINGDOM

The prophetic intercessor is an intercessor who has been enabled by the Spirit to create birth-openings. Just as when a woman gives birth and the contractions and pangs create an opening that is adequate for the birth process, so do our prophetic declarations create openings for the Kingdom. We wrestle in prayer until our objective has been achieved. We cannot give up.

The opening process requires persistence. Prophetic intercessors will even pray to increase their own ability to pray. They will pray for more effective "contractions" and for more unction. They will wrestle down anything that tries to close down the opening, such as unbelief or false beliefs. (For example, "I am a second-class citizen...I have nothing to contribute.")

Even after my children were born, I kept on contending for them. I think most mothers do this. We become like she-bears, defending the lives to which we have given birth. Therefore it should be no surprise to see that an intercessor contends like that for the life of the Kingdom that he or she is responsible for birthing. Intercessors carry life and bring it to birth and keep protecting it from harm.

Prophetic intercessors will spot the gaps and go stand in them. They will be able to identify gifts that are missing and release them. If a certain Kingdom-birthing requires a gift of evangelism they will declare it, and the same goes for any other gift. Teachers, apostles, more prophets, and so on will be freed to step forward.

As prophetic intercessors, we can hold each other up in prayer. We can nurture each other whether or not we have had physical children to nurture. With devoted prayer, we can create shortcuts for each other by allowing the Lord to take our struggles and do His redemptive work, transforming them into silver and gold—treasures that we can pass on to someone else so that they will not have to go through all the things that we have had to go through.

In picture language, the Church is the Bride of Christ. And as His Bride, it is as if we have a womb into which the Lord can plant His seeds. Sometimes, what He plants may not grow up the way we expected, but we are privileged to welcome each new aspect of the Kingdom and nurture it, spirit to Spirit. As sons and daughters of our Father, we can ask Him for help every step of the way. Shouldering the work of prophetic intercession, we find new meaning in passages from Scripture such as this one:

> For as many as are led by the Spirit of God, these are sons of God. For you did not receive the spirit of bondage again to fear, but you received the Spirit of adoption by whom we cry out, "Abba, Father." The Spirit Himself bears witness with our spirit that we are children of God, and if children, then heirs—heirs of God and joint heirs with Christ, if indeed we suffer with Him, that we may also be glorified together. For I consider that the sufferings of this present time are not worthy to be compared with the glory which shall be revealed in

us. For the earnest expectation of the creation eagerly waits for the revealing of the sons of God. ...For we know that the whole creation groans and labors with birth pangs together until now. Not only that, but we also who have the firstfruits of the Spirit, even we ourselves groan within ourselves, eagerly waiting for the adoption, the redemption of our body. ...Likewise the Spirit also helps in our weaknesses. For we do not know what we should pray for as we ought, but the Spirit Himself makes intercession for us with groanings which cannot be uttered. Now He who searches the hearts knows what the mind of the Spirit is, because He makes intercession for the saints according to the will of God (Romans 8:14-19,22-23,26-27).

MY HEART IS YOUR HEART

Like the wind, the Spirit blows wherever He wishes, and if we are prophetic intercessors, so do we (see John 3:8). Like sailboats, we must tack this way and that in order to keep moving. God does not normally lead us by a direct path, although His chosen path will slice through whatever is in the way. As we put ourselves into His hands, we trust that He has chosen us for His purposes and that He can do anything. He can make good things out of bad things. He is more than able.

His way of doing things is not only good, it takes us on an adventure better than any ride at an amusement park. We ride with Him—twists and turns, upside down, screaming our heads off—and then we say, "Let's do it again, Daddy! Let's do it again!"

As we unite our hearts to His, we begin to blend together with Him. Our give and take and our ebb and flow become almost seamless, so that we no longer know where He ends and where we begin—and that's the way He wants it. As prophetic intercessors, we become new creations filled with the testimony of His goodness, confident that wherever He takes us it will be good. That has been part of my adventure into the prophetic—the wedding of the revelatory gifts of the Holy Spirit and the heart of prayer—to birth God's purposes in the earth.

Part Three

Purposes of the Prophetic Today

R eading each of the chapters in this book is like taking a peek through a new door. Each new "room" is different, and yet they are part of the same house.

As you conclude your tour through the house called *Adventures in the Prophetic*, you will explore in the next chapters some of the primary purposes of the prophetic today, complete with more firsthand accounts of the power of the prophetic to bring Heaven to earth so that God's warrior Bride, the Church, can outwit the enemy and help to bring in a great harvest.

The diversity of the prophetic is beyond description, just as God Himself is bigger and better than words can describe. Unlimited by gender, age, and even gifting, the prophetic life is an adventure that any and all of us can undertake. Ready, set, go!

Chapter 8

EARTHING THE PROPHETIC, BRINGING HEAVEN TO EARTH

Ryan Wyatt

When Jesus started His ministry, one of the first words out of his mouth was, *"Repent, for the Kingdom of Heaven is at hand"* (see Mark 1:15). He had brought the Kingdom with Him when He arrived, and He brought a heavenly government with him, too. That Kingdom and government never left the earth, although He did.

In fact, almost immediately He began to release it to the first generation of His disciples:

> *These twelve Jesus sent out and commanded them, saying:* *"Do not go into the way of the Gentiles, and do not enter a* *city of the Samaritans. But go rather to the lost sheep of the* *house of Israel. And as you go,* ***preach, saying, 'The King-*** ***dom of Heaven is at hand.'*** *Heal the sick, cleanse the lepers,* *raise the dead, cast out demons...* (Matthew 10:5-8).

Then after He died and rose from the dead, He spent 40 more days with His disciples before He ascended into Heaven. He told them more about the Kingdom of God, and He equipped them with His Holy Spirit so they too could demonstrate the Kingdom on earth.

Jesus did not come to earth to restore the Kingdom for a span of only a few years of public ministry, only to take it back with Him when He ascended. He did not come so that only a few people could be saved from hell and join Him in Heaven. Although He is going to return to earth again, bringing a greater dimension of the Kingdom with Him, His intention all along was that His Body here on earth would truly represent Him after He returned to the Father. He wanted to bring Heaven to earth in a decisive, dramatic way, leaving behind a Body of believers who would perform signs and wonders and who would continue to demonstrate the Kingdom to generations of people yet unborn.

"It's Time for the Prophetic to Be Earthed"

Not long ago, I felt that the Lord spoke to me very clearly. He said, "Ryan, it's time for the prophetic to be earthed." That was an unusual way to put it, but I knew He meant that He wanted the Church to begin to embody the Kingdom more than before, demonstrating the power and the government of the Kingdom in prophetic word and in action that validates and demonstrates the reality of the prophetic.

From firsthand experience, I knew already that a lot of people want to learn how to move in prophecy or words of knowledge or even how to perform signs and wonders. But too often their efforts are short-term. They are able to hop on board for a season, but then something always seems to happen; their attempts are always fleeting. It is as if people are riding a roller coaster of the Spirit. How on earth can the prophetic be "earthed" if the citizens of the Kingdom are going up and down so much?

This is not an impossible dream, but to fulfill it, people are going to have to fully embrace the message of the Kingdom, which will change them from spectators into participants. When people can become situated in a place of solid Kingdom identity, the prophetic gift will flow in a pure and consistent way. The apostolic and the prophetic come together when the prophetic is earthed with tangible demonstrations of the Kingdom. Instead of providing a place of visitation for God (which, as good as it is, is only temporary), the people of God will become a *habitation* for Him. New wineskins will be created that can carry His new wine to a new generation on a thirsty planet.

More than the Gospel of Salvation

The whole purpose of Jesus' ministry was *not* just to save people so He could take them to Heaven. That is the gospel of salvation, and there is nothing wrong with it except that it is just a piece of the Gospel of the Kingdom. Jesus did not preach the gospel of salvation. When we re-read His words in the Gospels, we soon realize that He came to preach the Gospel of the *Kingdom.*

Most of the Body of Christ adheres to the Gospel as they have been taught about it, and they have been taught a gospel of salvation. The message is limited: Get saved enough to get into Heaven—get your bus ticket to go home to Heaven. While you're here, you might as well be faithful to a church, pay your tithe, and listen to some good preaching so you can become a good disciple and develop godly character. All those things are good and noble things to do, but they only scratch the surface of the fullness of the Gospel of the Kingdom. It is like getting a ticket to a theme park and never going on any of the rides but instead camping out in the welcome center.

Living according to a salvation-only gospel means you are operating in a fraction of your inheritance. Yes, you are supposed to inherit Heaven one day, but the reality is that God is looking for people who are saved enough to bring Heaven to earth right now. Jesus is looking for people who will continue His work, which was to preach the Kingdom and to destroy the works of the devil seven days and nights a week, not only on the seventh day (see 1 John 3:8).

For the most part, I do not believe that the devil is highly threatened with the typical "Sunday Morning Christianity" mind-set. I have nothing against Sundays, but for most people their Sunday morning meetings become the extent of their Christianity. The devil will never be threatened by people who are just saved enough to get into Heaven. He likes them that way, because they are blissfully unaware of their purpose on earth. They figure that if they can just be good Christians and hang on to Jesus as they go through life, if they can be good, upstanding Christian citizens who are good role models for their kids, then it's OK if the world goes to hell in a hand basket because Jesus will come and sweep them up to Heaven before it's too late.

The trouble is, that does not line up with what we read in the Bible. What we read there, especially what Jesus says, is that we are supposed to continue doing what He did. Before Jesus Christ returns to the earth for the second time, He is first going to come "to us and through us" to display Himself to the world. He has deposited His Spirit into millions and even billions of people all over the earth so that together we could form a corporate Body of Jesus Christ for all the people of the world to see. If anything, our impact should be greater than what Jesus could make when He walked the earth as a man. In fact, He said, *"Greater works than these will* [you] *do,"* and the end of John's Gospel depicts even Jesus' solo works as so numerous that all the books of the world could not contain the account of them (see John 14:12; 21:25). It does not seem possible, but together the Body of Christ is meant to accomplish greater works in every way.

Kingdom Identity, Kingdom Atmosphere

We are supposed to know our identity as sons of God and effective members of the Body of Christ, but we don't. The enemy is taking advantage of this, and he is operating in a mantle of authority that no longer belongs to him. The mantle belongs to us. When we begin to assume our Kingdom role and identity, we will be able to take our place as Jesus' bodily representatives on the earth.

When Jesus walked the earth, he carried His own weather system with Him. He carried His own atmosphere. Faith rose and demons cried out when He stepped into view. When we rise up in our true identity, we, too, will carry a Kingdom atmosphere with us. No longer so affected by everything around us, we will begin to make a difference. When we walk into a room, we will no longer be a thermometer that registers everyone else's temperature. Instead, we will be a thermostat that will set the temperature.

A prime example of the apostolic and prophetic coming together was when the Word—something that is supernaturally prophetic—became flesh. The prophetic was earthed:

> *And the Word became flesh and dwelt among us, and we beheld His glory, the glory as of the only begotten of the Father, full of grace and truth. ...And of His fullness we have all received, and grace for grace. For the law was given through Moses, but grace and truth came through Jesus Christ* (John 1:14,16-17).

He dwelt among us. He unpacked His gifts. He made His habitation with us, and He tabernacled among us, giving the earth back to us because it is part of our inheritance; He gave us dominion over the earth so that we could be a demonstration of the Kingdom here on earth.

Several years ago, I experienced a visitation from the Lord that began this paradigm shift for me. I was in a hotel room by myself when suddenly the temperature of the room changed, becoming very, very warm. I went to check the thermostat, but it was not even on. Suddenly, the fear of the Lord gripped me and I felt His tangible presence. I went and sat down. I began to weep and to vibrate from the inside out. It felt very different from other vision-type encounters I have had. I became aware that He was coming—literally coming into the room.

Immediately, Jesus walked in from around the corner of my room, and He walked right up to me. He was dripping with oil from head to toe. As He came and stood next to me (where I was working hard just to stay in my chair), some of the oil came off on me. I remember sitting there, literally wiping my clothes and oil was on them, wiping my hair and oil was on it, wiping my face and oil was all over it.

He spoke. He said, "Ryan, this is the oil of the overcomer. I am releasing it in this hour for those who will begin to position themselves for it." Then He went on to say, "I am desperately hungry that I would have a people who will lay hold of their full inheritance…. I and I alone am your inheritance…. I and I alone am to be your possession" (see Ezek. 44:28).

Jesus also said to me, "I am desperately hungry that I would have My full inheritance in my people." For the first time, I really began to understand the fact that Jesus has an inheritance as well. His inheritance is not just born-again believers. He took me to the third chapter of Ephesians where Paul was speaking about the Church, about how *the manifold wisdom of God might be made known by the church to the principalities and powers in the heavenly places* (Eph. 3:10). The "manifold wisdom of God" refers to all of who God is—His character, His love, His presence, His power. Through the Church, He wants to display all of who He is, so that the powers of darkness will be supplanted by His Light.

That is His inheritance. He does not want to have a beat-up, bruised, and broken-but-saved Bride who will join Him someday in Heaven. He wants to have a powerful, victorious, effective warrior Bride who is demonstrating her unity with His victory on the Cross and who is occupying and advancing the Kingdom until He comes.

That is what He was modeling when the Word became flesh and dwelt among us so we could see His glory. The prophetic Word was "earthed" in the most earthly way—by being conceived in the womb of a young woman and born as a baby. The angel Gabriel came to Mary and said, "You are going to conceive in your womb and bring forth the Christ child" (see Luke 1:31-33). She wondered aloud how this could possibly occur because she was a virgin. And the angel said, in essence, "Oh, don't worry. The Holy Spirit is going to overshadow you and the power of the Most High is going to come upon you." Her 23 chromosomes were going to be joined by the incorruptible DNA of God. It was a tangible transaction. It was not just a nice, hypothetical story.

Mary carried the Christ child, the God-man, for nine months as He grew inside her. And then she gave birth to Him. He was born into a birth family on earth. He was "earthed." He did not arrive in a chariot or materialize out of thin air.

More than that, His conception and birth showed us how we, too, could be regenerated, reborn, how the very seed of God could come into us. "He who is joined to the Lord is one spirit with Him" (1 Cor. 6:17). This is deeper than we realize. I have heard people teach that we are like a New Testament ark of the covenant. That is a good thought, but we are more than a mere container for the Holy Spirit—we are new creatures in Christ. Our spirit has been infused with His.

We have not merely assented to a creed and joined a social club. We have God's DNA in us, and it has transformed our nature at its core. It is as if our umbilical cords have been unplugged from the line of Adam and plugged into the last Adam, Jesus (see 1 Cor. 15:45). We are no longer citizens of the earth; we are citizens of the Kingdom of Heaven. Paul put it this way:

> *Do you not know that you are the temple of God and that the Spirit of God dwells in you?...For the temple of God is holy, which temple you are* (1 Corinthians 3:16-17).

KINGDOM COLONIZATION

Our primary citizenship is now in the Kingdom of Heaven. This has almost become a cliché. What should it mean to us? It should mean that we are fulfilling part of God's plan—to colonize the earth.

We can understand colonization by looking at what the Romans did. They would create what they called "little Romes" wherever they took territory. They would move, say, three hundred people from Rome. Some of them would be warriors, some would be carpenters, some blacksmiths, some chefs, and so on—all kinds of people. They would move them to whatever faraway place they had just conquered, and they would instruct them to live according to the culture of Rome there. Even though they had been transplanted into a culture that was nothing like Rome, they were to import Rome into the new territory. So they would live according to the Roman economy; they would eat Roman food, dress in Roman clothes, and speak Latin. Before long, they would have an influence. They could spread out from their colony and take over more territory.

You can see the parallel. The Church on the earth can be likened to a colony of Heaven. Citizens of the Kingdom of Heaven are living in foreign territory. Not only do they retain their Kingdom mind-set and rule system, they also demonstrate the culture of the Kingdom of Heaven. By living there, they change the place so that it becomes "on earth as it is in Heaven."

Jesus taught His disciples to pray, *"Our Father in Heaven, hallowed be Your name. Your Kingdom come. Your will be done on earth as it is in Heaven"* (Matt. 6:9-10). He added, a little later, comments about how He had given them the power and authority they needed to bring His Kingdom to earth (see Matt. 10). If you stop and think about it, you realize that up to this point the disciples did not yet have the indwelling Holy Spirit, although they did have an external anointing that helped them minister. They still had Jesus with them in the flesh instead of having the internal, resident Christ inside, bringing them the hope of glory. And yet they were starting to colonize their part of the earth already.

The Earth as Our Inheritance

The point I am trying to get across is that the members of the Body of Christ are one with the Holy Spirit, who is the most powerful supernatural force on the earth.

God formed the man from the dust of the ground and He created human beings with the capacity to be multidimensional so that He could release the invisible realm into the visible realm. From the very beginning, He intended for His sons to live on the earth, to have dominion, to be fruitful and multiply. He wanted them to spread the lifestyle of walking with Him in the cool of the day. He wanted them to demonstrate the Kingdom.

The body that He created from the dust of the ground came equipped with five natural senses: sight, hearing, smell, touch, and taste. Those senses make it possible for human beings to interact with the natural realm around them and to undertake the responsibilities of their delegated authority. From the very beginning, God did not create men and women for Heaven; He created them for both earth and Heaven. Creating them with both heavenly and earthly substance, He made them multidimensional, with bodies and with spirits, so they could live on the earth and demonstrate the rule of Heaven. God said:

> "Let Us make man in Our image, according to Our likeness; let them have dominion over the fish of the sea, over the birds of the air, and over the cattle, over all the earth and over every creeping thing that creeps on the earth." So God created man in His own image; in the image of God He created him; male and female He created them. Then God blessed them, and God said to them, "Be fruitful and multiply; fill the earth and subdue it; have dominion over the fish of the sea, over the birds of the air, and over every living thing that moves on the earth" (Genesis 1:26-28).

So there was Adam in this earth suit. And God breathed into his nostrils the breath of life so that he could become a living creature. When He breathed that breath of life into Adam, He was breathing the very essence of Himself into Adam's spirit. God did not breathe the Holy Spirit into Adam; He breathed His very essence into Adam, forming Adam's human spirit.

To this day, each human being comes equipped with a body, a soul, and a spirit. Every single human being on the earth has a human spirit. Now the fact of the matter is that unbelievers have a weakened, empty spirit. It is not inhabited by the Holy Spirit. Nobody is home. They can still operate in the spirit realm but not in the Kingdom of God. But believers have spirits that have come alive to God and His Kingdom.

The words of the Book of Genesis tell us that human beings were created in the image of God (see Gen. 1:26). This does not mean we were created to look like Him, but it does mean that we were created to *be* like Him. That should not be too hard for us to understand, because each of us was born of parents and we are a lot like them whether we want to be or not. We may resemble them physically, but we are not carbon copies.

There is a part of you right now that has always existed (your human spirit) because God breathed it into you from His very essence. You have always existed, in God. That is why all of humanity cries out for Him, because that human spirit craves to be filled with God. That is why we are all multidimensional human beings, even unbelievers. And that is why unbelievers can actually manifest supernatural power if they want to. The devil is on a full-force campaign to release a counterfeit power of God to fascinate people. Whether they realize that they are worshiping satan or not, the world is hungry for the supernatural.

As Kingdom citizens, we have the real Spirit, the One with Kingdom authority. We carry the glory of God inside us. That glory is multidimensional, too. The glory of God activates us in revelation, using our spiritual senses. It gives us power and authority. The glory brings us into intimacy and closeness with the One who is the source of life. It fascinates us, woos us, and transforms us. The Holy Spirit dwelling within our spirits gives us identity. Malachi wrote: *"...The Lord, whom you seek, will suddenly come to His temple, even the Messenger of the covenant, in whom you delight. Behold, He is coming"* (Mal. 3:1). What is His temple? We are His temple. He is coming and He is here, creating a holy place that carries the holy atmosphere of heavenly culture.

When God created the first man and woman, He was making a prototype for the whole human race, for the multitudes of people who would populate the earth, living in union and intimacy with Him and having dominion over the planet. That was the original plan. Adam was never intended to die. Sin was never intended to mar the picture. There was no curse on the earth at all.

Adam and Eve lived in a place where Heaven and earth were overlapping. The man and the woman were agents, stewards of the Kingdom of Heaven on the earth. They were people of signs and wonders. They did not have to toil or suffer pain. They carried a mantle of glory and authority over their shoulders that was so powerful that when they dropped it, they still had a relationship with God. Like many believers who have a salvation level of relationship with God, they lost the glory but they did not lose the Lord of glory.

Habitation of Glory

When Adam threw that mantle off he set off a civil war in Heaven. A governmental regime change occurred. That mantle of authority that Adam had unknowingly spurned was picked up and placed onto the devil's shoulders. Authority over the earth was turned over to the usurper. Satan began to operate as the god of this world, to the point that when Jesus was tempted in the wilderness, he could rightfully claim to be the one who could bestow authority over the earthly realm (see Matt. 4:8-9; Luke 4:5-6). Far from being just a sad story about how Adam and Even lost a level of intimacy with God, the Fall was a regime change of monumental proportions, one that would require the life of the Son of God to set it right.

Ever since Jesus' sinless life, His death, and His resurrection, the mantle of authority has been restored to redeemed human beings, but most of us have not realized it. Since we do not realize who we are in Christ and we do not step into our true identity and authority, the devil still occupies that role. We leave it vacant, so he steps right in. *"We know that we are of God, and that the whole world lies in the power of the evil one"* (1 John 5:19 NASB). Even though conditionally satan does not carry that mantle anymore, experientially he does—until we begin to operate in our rightful, God-given authority.

We have all of biblical history to show us God's plan. From early times, He began to foreshadow His desire to gather a group of people together so that His glory could find habitation in their midst. He chose Israel, pulling them out of bondage in Egypt (which is like believers being born again and delivered from bondage, removed from the kingdom of darkness and brought into the Kingdom of Light). As they roamed the wilderness, God began to demonstrate to them a new culture of the Kingdom. He spoke with Moses directly and He gave him the Law.

It wasn't God's full plan just to save them from Egypt (being born again). God intended them to enter their Promised Land in their lifetime, but to do it He had to change the people themselves and introduce them to an entirely new culture—a supernatural culture of the Kingdom. The people began to obey. Their lifestyle changed. The new culture took over. God was trying to demonstrate a heavenly, supernatural cultural model. He stayed with them in the form of a pillar of cloud and a pillar of fire. He was showing them how to create a dwelling place for His glory to abide in their midst.

The Book of Galatians indicates that the Law was given as a "tutor" (see Gal. 3:24). God was trying to protect Israel until the Perfect One could come. Until the fullness of that time could be reached, God was going to keep a nation of people for Himself, and He was going to teach them about hosting the glory of God in their midst. The other nations did not love the people of Israel, but they respected them. Because it was a known fact that God was dwelling with them as a pillar of cloud and a pillar of fire, the other nations did not disregard them.

The World Wants the Living Jesus

There is inherent power in the written Word of God, and yet the words are meant to lead people to the Living Word, Jesus. Jesus told the Pharisees and the Sadducees, who were devoted to the Law:

> *You search the Scriptures because you think that in them*
> *you have eternal life; it is these that testify about Me; and*

you are unwilling to come to Me so that you may have life (John 5:39-40 NASB).

The power that is inherent in the universal truths expressed in the Word is available to anybody who wants to use it. Some New Agers use the words of the Bible to greater effect than most believers do. New York Times bestsellers have been written about positive thinking (*"Set your mind on things above…"* Col. 3:2) and reaping what you sow. Even as the Kingdom culture infuriates the devil and the people he influences, it is attractive to those whose spirits God created.

We cannot say that the world does not want Jesus simply because they seem to reject Him. The world wants the *living* Jesus. They wanted the living Jesus when He walked the earth and they want the living Jesus now. All they could say was, *"Who is this who speaks with such authority?"* (see Luke 4:36). Even when He was not doing miracles—and He did not do signs and wonders every minute—something about Him made people want to be with Him. He carried the atmosphere of Heaven. He told the people, *"… The words that I speak to you are spirit, and they are life"* (John 6:63). When Jesus spoke, His words filled the room with a heavenly presence. His words were capsules of Spirit, capsules of life.

They still are. I have been in meetings in which I simply opened my Bible and began to speak about Moses and the glory of God, and later witches came forward from the back where they had been trying to curse the meeting. They came up at the end of the meeting to ask, "What is that blue light that would come off the pages and out of your mouth when you talked about the glory of God?"

There is no substitute for the Living Word of God.

The DNA of the Father

Because we carry the DNA of our Father in Heaven individually and corporately, we are by definition people who carry the glory of God, people who perform signs and wonders and who live out of the fullness of their inheritance here and now on earth.

God's purpose for the Church as the corporate Body/Bride of Christ is for her to display the Kingdom of God just as Jesus did when He walked the earth as an individual person. He displayed the Kingdom and so should we. Although humanity was handicapped greatly by the repercussions of the failure of our forefather Adam, God has pursued His purpose relentlessly, manifesting Himself to and through the prophet-and-priest culture of Israel, tabernacling with His people, and eventually sending His Son to redeem people for His Kingdom and remove the handicaps inherited from the first Adam.

As the Body of Christ, we are now the royal priesthood (a reflection of the priesthood of the tribe of Levi), operating as mediators between Heaven and earth. The Church of Jesus Christ is now the holy nation of God. Citizens of the Kingdom of Heaven, we are colonizing the earth, importing a culture of heavenly glory wherever we find ourselves.

How does this play out in our lives? I will give you an example that may seem to be exceptional, but I think it should be more common among us. I was getting ready to minister in New York City, and I went into a trance. (A trance is like a Holy Ghost anesthesia. When you are in a trance—as Peter was when he had the vision of unclean foods in Acts 10—God shows you things you might not be able to accept if He didn't put you into a trance first.)

When I was in the trance, I had a vision in which a young woman walked up to me and told me her name and different things about her life. After the vision ended, the Lord said, "I want you to call her out by name in the meeting and then prophesy to her; it will be a sign and a wonder."

Her name was an odd one and the church was a French sidewalk church in the East Village neighborhood in Manhattan. So I was supposed to call out this person by a very unique name in a group of only 40 or 50 people. When you call out someone's name in a larger meeting, you stand more likelihood of getting close to the right name, so this felt risky. But

I went ahead and did it that evening. Sure enough, thank God, she was there! I delivered the prophetic word, remembering that the Lord had said there would be a miracle because of this.

As I spoke out the word to the young woman, I could feel a tangible glory coming from behind me and passing through me, and the instant it passed through me, tears shot from my eyes. Then the glory hit the young woman, who, as it turned out, hardly ever came to church but just happened to be there that day. She was far from God, living with two men. I never got close enough to touch her, but the glory of God hit her so powerfully that she went down to the ground. The power went back about ten rows and you could see it touch row after row; people would just begin to weep as it hit their row. The effect of the glory stopped at about the tenth row.

At the end of the meeting, a lady walked up and I remembered having seen her in about the tenth row. She said, "I am one of the most powerful New Agers in East Village. I am a local palm reader. Everybody knows me." She said, "I know spiritual power, and what I experienced here today, I think it might have been love." She didn't know for sure because, as she said, "I never in my life have experienced power like that. That's greater power than I have ever operated in. I have decided that I want to know this Jesus."

You see, the presence of God's glory was like a substance in that place. All I did was to be available, to come into the place obediently, and to invite Him to do His work. The presence of the glory of God's Kingdom is like an overshadowing when God's DNA infuses human nature with His. The signs and wonders that result from the exercise of the prophetic gift are byproducts of the glory of God, activated by His Spirit.

All we have to do is to be available. We worship Him. We enter into His presence. We welcome Him and we welcome whatever manifestation of life He chooses to bring with Him. As we do so, soaking in His glory, He releases us further from the bonds of earth, and we find identity as His sons and daughters, people of signs and wonders. No longer do we suffer from condemnation or a shame mentality. No longer must we battle through extra spiritual warfare because of our performance mentality. We display Kingdom life because we are blood relatives of the King. We belong to Him and He wants to give us His Kingdom.

People who hunger and thirst for the essence of God will be satisfied. God will overshadow them. They will be marked with His substance and transformed by His glory, able to manifest His life wherever they find themselves. The Kingdom will be earthed.

Chapter 9

Prophetic Strategy in Spiritual Warfare
Mickey Robinson

The devil's plan is to discourage you from God's plan, especially if you are pressing in to do what you believe God wants you to do. He wants to blanket you with lies and distractions so he can drown out the voice of God in your life.

But you need to know that the devil cannot stop God from speaking. As hard as he tries, he cannot get ahead of God's strategies. God will continue to communicate His encouragement and His Kingdom strategies to you, and as long as you keep on listening, you will know what you are supposed to do.

"Keep Them from the Evil One"

Jesus initiated a relationship with each one of us, and He wants to keep us close to Himself, so close that He can trust us with His Kingdom strategies. Take a fresh look at what He told His Father about His relationship with us:

> *I have manifested Your name to the men whom You have given Me out of the world. They were Yours, You gave them*

*to Me, and they have kept Your word. ...For I have given to
them the words which You have given Me; and they have
received them, and have known surely that I came forth
from You; and they have believed that You sent Me. I pray
for them. I do not pray for the world but for those whom
You have given Me, for they are Yours. ...Holy Father, keep
through Your name those whom You have given Me, that
they may be one as We are* (John 17:6,8-9,11).

Improbable as it may seem, the Son of God has initiated a relationship
with each one of us, and He intends to protect and sustain it. To do so, He
will continue to give us the words of life that His Father gives to Him. Our
part is to follow Him and to receive His words eagerly.

Therefore, our guiding principle for spiritual warfare should be main-
taining a healthy relationship with the Father, Son, and Holy Spirit. The
degree and quality of the prophetic revelation you receive has much more
to do with your relationship with God than it does with your gifting. Your
relationship with God is based on ongoing, active communication (without which any relationship will wither). You can be related to a person, but
you cannot claim to have a true relationship with that person unless you
have some kind of mutual interaction. An inactive relationship is too weak
to be conducive to deep sharing of important information.

You Need Firsthand Revelation

People often quote Proverbs 29:18 in the King James Version: *"Where
there is no vision, the people perish."* Other versions translate the word for
"perish" as "unrestrained" (see the New American Standard Bible, the New
International Version, and the New King James Version). In other words,
in the absence of revelation—which means prophetic words or messages
from God—people will do whatever they feel like doing. Even when their
actions throw everything out of balance, they will not be able to choose
life-giving behavior or make good decisions. That is why people need to
hear from God on an ongoing basis.

Whose fault is it when people fail to hear God's voice? All of us have been in difficult situations that made us ask, "Where is God in all this?" As we always find out, God has never moved. He is always present in every situation. But to recognize Him, and especially to hear what He's saying in the midst of it, you need to understand who you are in relationship to Him, and you have to keep fanning the flame of the Spirit in your life.

As the seasons of life turn, you may not feel close to God every minute, but you can still hear His voice. Much of the time you will have the support of other people, but sometimes you will be on your own with God. If you can't hear His voice then, you will really be in trouble.

In First Samuel 14, we read about a time when Saul's son Jonathan was on his own, accompanied only by his armor bearer. The two of them left Saul and his six hundred men in the valley and they struck out on their own, sneaking up on a garrison of the Philistine army with only one sword between them—and a lot of faith. Jonathan had felt led to venture up the mountain to take on the Philistines who held the pass. To prove that this was what God wanted to do, he instructed his armor bearer to come out into the open with him where their enemies could see them. The two of them would present themselves in plain sight of the Philistines, and if their enemies invited them to come up, they would take it as a sign that God was going to give them victory in hand-to-hand combat. That is exactly what happened, against military logic and even common sense, and God got all the credit for the victory.

That maneuver took courage and rock-solid confidence—in God, not in human plans or weaponry. Jonathan did not trust in his own strength. He ventured out on a series of prophetic senses. His strategy came straight from God, and in order to have the necessary faith to carry it off, he had to hear from God at every step of the way. He knew he belonged to God and that his relative weakness would be made strong in God's plan.

MEEK AND POWERFUL

When we approach warfare the way Jonathan did, with humble confidence in the outstanding wisdom and strength of the Lord, we can prevail over our enemies. No longer do we have to use valuable energy parrying their attacks. Instead, we can take the offense and execute a plan of God's devising. Like Moses, a "meek" man whose humility and trust made it possible for God to use him to deliver a nation, we submit to the hand of God and watch Him work (see Num. 12:3 AMP).

It is simple: If you want to find yourself on the winning side, you need to submit to God. Humility is the strong fortress of all godly people. You can be humble and yet completely bold because your confidence is not in yourself. It is in the strongest power of all. You need to put on humility, because, as Scripture says, *"God resists the proud, but gives grace to the humble"* (James 4:6). And, as Peter added, *"Therefore humble yourselves under the mighty hand of God, that He may exalt you in due time"* (1 Pet. 5:6).

Note that it is your responsibility to humble yourself. That is your job. It is God's responsibility to exalt you. So if you decide to exalt yourself, you are usurping God's job, and God will say, "OK, if you want to do My job, I'll do yours." You really do not want God to humble you. He is very good at it.

Moses humbled himself. In fact, the Bible tells us that he was the meekest man on the face of the earth, and yet he marched up to Pharaoh, the ruler of the world superpower of the time, with nothing but his shepherd's staff. Moses said confidently, "I have been sent from my God. I have a word for you: 'Let My people go.' Let your economic system go, the system that has thrived upon four centuries of slavery of the Jewish people. I am here by myself but I represent a God who appeared to me as a burning bush who is saying, 'Let My people go.'" (See Exodus 5.)

But as he heard the words spoken by Moses, Pharaoh hardened his heart. This strange shepherd-man Moses was very foolish if he thought he could persuade a mighty pharaoh to change his mind.

Then Moses started prophesying about the troubles that would ensue. Egyptians considered frogs divine and they worshiped them. So Moses said, "You like frogs? How about a couple of billion of them? Frogs in your living room, frogs in the cupboard. Frogs in the cookie jar. Frogs in your beer. Frogs dying and filling the streets so that people are stepping on them. Frogs everywhere."

And that was just one of ten plagues. Plague after plague hit the nation of Egypt. Finally, Pharaoh relented and let the people of Israel go.

You see, Moses did not focus on the powerful opposition of his enemies, and neither should we. He obeyed God and kept listening to Him. Most people can't help but focus on undoing evil first. But you need to wage war between your two ears first, then submit to God and get your marching orders. Only His strategies will work.

When you get darkness out of your thought life—the things such as fears and insecurities—the truth will set you free. Jesus is praying for you. He said, *"I pray for them. I do not pray for the world but for those whom You have given Me, for they are Yours,"* and *"...keep them from the evil one"* (John 17:9,15). Because of Jesus, you are already farther up the ladder than you thought you were.

When you start thinking, "If only I were more famous or more anointed," you can recognize those thoughts as mind games from the dark spirit, and you can counter with the information that what makes *you* strong and famous is your relationship with God. His personal love for you makes you stronger than all worldly fame or wealth.

Some of the strongest people I know do not use earthly titles of authority. They simply use their own first and last names. They tend to use the name of Jesus more than they do their own. They do not do that to sound spiritual or religious but rather because they have a love relationship with this man Jesus and it is so real that they cannot help but talk about the One they love so much. They have taken up residence in the safe stronghold of humility, and their own names are not even on the door.

So keep the conversation going. Listen to Him. Your effectiveness and your happiness depend on your relationship with Him. As you hear God say things to you, you will feel His love pouring into your heart and you will know that His truth is setting you free.

COMBATING ENEMY STRATEGY

Your own humble submission to God will foil the enemy's four-pronged strategy against believers.

The devil usually starts by leveling some form of *discouragement* at you. Something will go wrong—maybe in a relationship, maybe on your job, maybe on the news, maybe in your church—and you will start to get discouraged. Remember, discouragement is the opposite of encouragement, which comes with prophetic words from the Spirit of God. The enemy has a degree of understanding about you and your destiny and he wants to undermine it, so he sends the opposite spirit.

After discouragement comes *confusion*. Even the things you thought you knew for sure will seem shaky. You will waver, "Maybe I was wrong." Your life will seem to be going out of control.

After confusing you for a while, the enemy can deprive you of your *vision*. Without a vision of the Kingdom of God and of your own prophetic life-purpose, all you can see are the temporary things of this world, including your obligations and responsibilities. You lose sight of your true heavenly vision and you begin to think things like this: "I should take a little time for myself, maybe play some golf or go away for a while. I should concentrate on making some money...." When this happened to the apostle Peter, he said, *"I will go back to being a fisherman"* (see John 21:3). He lost his vision for being a world-changer, the first disciple to confess Jesus as the Christ. After he failed the Lord and denied knowing Him, he went from discouragement to confusion to loss of vision in less than two months. The same man who had left his livelihood to follow Jesus, the one who had walked on water and who had seemed to be bold all the time, simply returned to the safety of the family business.

As Peter did after his loss of vision, so do we: backing off from others, *withdrawing* from the company of people who might be able to restore us. We stay away from the things that used to energize us. We drop relationships which means we stop having fellowship. The things that used to interest us seem boring.

Discouragement, confusion, loss of vision, withdrawal—does this sound at all familiar? When you fall prey to this sort of attack, what can you do about it?

You can start by remembering some basic truth. Open your Bible and just start reading, or ask a friend to tell you the truth. God will not snuff you out, even if you are a "smoldering wick" (see Matt. 12:20; Isa. 42:3). He wants to restore you and use you again. Your discouragement and loss of vision may have happened because of real events and real evil, but the Good Shepherd never changes. Take your eyes off the circumstances and put them back on Him. Ask Him to speak to you and restore your relationship. Jesus sought Peter out and spoke with him. Among other things, He told him how satan had demanded to sift him like wheat (see Luke 22:31).

What if satan has a legal right to sift you like wheat, as he did with Peter? Doesn't that seal your fate? No, Jesus has prayed for you ahead of time as He did for Peter, and He intercedes all the time for you. He lives forever to make intercession (see Heb. 7:25). Every prayer that is ever prayed goes through Him. He is a priest forever, and He has the power of an indestructible life (see Heb. 7:17). He never got elected and He's never going to resign. Nobody can take Him out of office. The government is on His shoulders, and yet He cares about your personal situation. Turn to Him. His nature is pure faithfulness, and He loves you.

WAITING FOR A WORD OF WISDOM

Some people consider the word of wisdom—one of the revelatory gifts of the Spirit—uninteresting compared to other gifts. I disagree. To me, the prophetic word of wisdom is highly dramatic because it is so powerful. Granted, it is often hidden from our view. Yet wisdom born from above represents a remarkable level of spiritual strategy. A word of wisdom can stop conflict before it happens. It can defuse tensions before they escalate, resolving impossible challenges.

Jesus spoke out words of wisdom all the time. Think about how He handled the situation when the woman caught in adultery was brought to Him or when the Pharisees tried to trap Jesus regarding paying taxes to Caesar (see John 8:1-11; Matt. 22:15-22). The best-known example of a word of wisdom in the Bible is the story of the two mothers who brought the baby to King Solomon (see 1 Kings 3:16-28).

When one of us receives a word of wisdom from God, we glimpse the Kingdom of Heaven. Considering how many conflicts we suffer, why don't we consult God more often? Waiting expectantly for a prophetic word of wisdom should become our primary Kingdom strategy for life. God is speaking all the time, you know. However, we do not listen enough, and sometimes we discount the insignificant-seeming words of wisdom that He sends us.

For example, my wife, Barbara, and I had a situation in the middle of the credit crunch. Two years before, we had moved to a new house and now we were supposed to renegotiate the terms of the loan—in one of the worst possible times to do so. Besides that, our financial situation is unusual, being self-employed in ministry. Banks were not loaning money even to wealthy people who had excellent credit. What were they going to do with us?

I took it to the Lord and He said, "Don't worry about it." That's it. Just "don't worry about it."

Sure enough, we got a good deal. But then it fell through, because the bank refused to buy our contract. I started to get a little worried. Maybe I should come up with another plan. Still, I remembered that God had said, "Don't worry about it." So I kept pressing in for another deal, believing God, being diligent but not anxious. As it worked out, somehow the value of our house went up just as the value of everyone else's was going down. The new loan had to take effect within a certain two-week period of time, which was one of the worst two weeks to negotiate such a deal, and yet our new house payment went down while the value of the house went up. I still don't know quite how that happened.

God's word of wisdom was simply "don't worry about it," and that was enough. He knew what He was going to do, and He didn't want me losing any sleep over it. I heard the word in my spirit and my spirit could tell my soul to expect God to take care of it. Holding onto the "don't worry about it" word, my spirit could tell my soul to be patient, even joyful, while waiting for the answer.

Think about similar experiences you have had. He has always come through for you, hasn't He? Even though His solutions are often much different from what you were expecting, He has done incredible things for you. While the devil tries to tell you that you are pinned against the wall with no way out, God just carves a doorway where there was no door, and you walk right through the wall. He sends His word of wisdom, simple and yet powerful, to help you.

REVELATION STOPS CONFLICT

You can see how revelation from God stops conflict before it gets started. When you combine a word of wisdom with holiness and a solid grasp of your status as a child of God, the enemy cannot lay hold of you. The devil cannot grab you or hold onto you. With the Spirit of Jesus actively living inside you, you can avoid many skirmishes that would otherwise turn into major battles.

Jesus said:

> *I will not talk with you much more, for the prince (evil genius, ruler) of the world is coming. And he has no claim on Me. [He has nothing in common with Me; there is nothing in Me that belongs to him, and he has no power over Me]* (John 14:30 AMP).

Jesus had no sins, no loose ends that satan could lay hold of. His holiness bought Him the time He needed to wait for a word of wisdom from His Father and to deliver it at just the right moment.

Remember how Jesus dealt with the woman who had been caught in adultery. He waited for a word of wisdom. By writing in the dirt, He bought some time. Then he uttered one short sentence, *"He who is without sin among you, let him throw a stone at her first"* (John 8:7). The woman's murderous accusers put down the stones they were about to hurl at her and slipped away. Conflict (and death by stoning) was averted. A life got redeemed. All through one word of wisdom.

None of us is as sinless as Jesus, but that does not mean that we cannot grow in our ability to elude the enemy, who tries to trap us in circumstances and make us say the wrong things in reaction to him. One way you can escape is to keep your mouth closed or pray silently in tongues instead of blurting out the first thing that comes to your mind. When you are under a personal attack or having a relationship problem, you need to hear from God. Don't open yourself up to the enemy by reacting with thoughts such as, "I can't stand this kind of person." Instead, pause and regroup. Take a deep breath and ask God to help you. Bypass your fleshly reactions in favor of responding with your spirit.

Scripture says, *"Agree with your adversary quickly…"* (Matt. 5:25). Sometimes you can do that. If the enemy is suggesting to your mind, "Yeah, you always make the same mistake, over and over," you can agree: "Yes, I do. But the Lord is my Shepherd and I shall not want. He is going to make things different this time."

When you do that, it shuts the enemy up. He wants you to start wrestling with him, but instead you are agreeing with him. You are responding with your spirit, and you are priming the pump for a word of wisdom.

You have been equipped with the mind of Christ (see 1 Cor. 2:16). That means you fit the profile of a man or woman of holiness, who shows *"by his good behavior his deeds in the gentleness of wisdom,"* and whose life is filled with mercy, steadiness, honesty, and other good fruit (see James 3:13,17-18 NASB).

JESUS BY YOUR SIDE

Jesus makes all the difference. Not only is He a good example, His Spirit ministers to you all the time. Having Jesus with you is better than receiving a personal word from a well-known Christian prophet. Having Jesus at his side made all the difference for Paul when he was facing heavy opposition. In the Book of Acts, Luke quotes Paul as saying:

> *Now I go bound in the spirit to Jerusalem, not knowing the things that will happen to me there, except that the Holy Spirit testifies in every city, saying that chains and tribulations await me. But none of these things move me; nor do I count my life dear to myself, so that I may finish my race with joy, and the ministry which I received from the Lord Jesus, to testify to the gospel of the grace of God (Acts 20:22-24).*

In city after city, Paul was hearing about these imminent trials through prophetic words. The Christians in these cities loved Paul, and they did not want to say goodbye to him or see him suffer. The Ephesians begged him not to go to Jerusalem. ("Stay here with us. We'll give you a condo, massages, organic food. We love you so much!") But he would not be deterred.

As far as he was concerned, the impending trials were supposed to happen; they must be part of the Lord's plan, especially since all of the words agreed. The people in different cities could not phone or e-mail each other to verify what had been prophesied in earlier venues. The Holy Spirit Himself was confirming His will through the series of prophetic. Paul took his leave of his friends, commending them to the care of the same Spirit who had spoken so many words about his destiny:

> *So now, brethren, I commend you to God and to the word of His grace, which is able to build you up and give you an inheritance among all those who are sanctified* (Acts 20:32).

Those prophetic words were fulfilled, and God's Kingdom advanced as a result. That was the whole point. Armed with God's words and setting his face like flint to obey, Paul defeated the enemy.

We too have the words of the Spirit of Jesus ringing in the ears of our spirits. While we may never face soldiers or rioting mobs of people, we have the same unseen enemy as Paul did, and we need to apply heavenly words of wisdom to our circumstances.

Often, as he tried to do in Ephesus and elsewhere, the enemy sneaks right into the Church, sowing fears and misdirection. I had an experience in the early 1980s that showed me how to apply the ever-present words of the Spirit to combat very subtle lies from the enemy in the Church. A very gifted pastor and teacher was challenging our congregation on the subject of rejection. Using many convincing Scriptures as proof, he really nailed the point that rejection was sin. Virtually everybody in our church went forward to repent. He made it sound inescapable. Everybody was guilty of the sin of rejection. Only if you had rebellion, denial, or spiritual blindness would you hold back. Well, I held back.

Not that I hadn't experienced rejection. I certainly had, much more than the average person. Having started out in an alcoholic, abusive home and then being in that plane crash where I was so horribly disfigured, I definitely knew what it was like to be rejected. I had been stripped of my human dignity, given up to die, and ever since I had noticed how people looked the other way when they encountered me. During the service, I thought about all of that rejection. I actually wanted to feel guilty and I wondered why I could not. Something must be wrong with me. Why did I not feel bad?

God explained it to me. He drew my attention to the fact that rejection opens wounds, which can in fact become areas of vulnerability to spiritual attack. In the midst of attack, we can fall prey to sin. But the rejection itself is not a sin. To consider rejection as sin would bring judgment against victims of child abuse, racial prejudice, or any other kind of prejudice and practically every type of uninvited social injustice that people have suffered since the beginning of time. Furthermore, not only was the concept of rejection as sin inaccurate, the guilt-driven, futile, powerless religious struggle to be set free by human efforts was even worse.

Abiding in Jesus had provided me with a place of safety and invulnerability. Knowing that I was part of the family of God, I had been delivered from rejection, which is a form of fear. What was I afraid of? I was not worried about who liked me or not, and I was not afraid of feeling rejected. None of that mattered, because I had been accepted by the only One who really matters.

I didn't feel guilty because I wasn't standing on common ground with the enemy where rejection was concerned. I had worked that one through. I was convinced of Jesus' love and acceptance through His written Word and through firsthand experience. Now I could hear in my heart a fresh word of wisdom for the moment. He was showing me that rejection itself was not a sin, so I could walk away free without participating in that altar call. I could press on in my desire to be eternally focused by listening to His voice.

THE FORTRESS OF FAITH

We can do nothing apart from God—nothing that makes a difference in this life and for eternity; it all comes about by faith. Concerning the realm of spiritual warfare, faith is often tested by fire; coming through the fire proves what kind of metal our faith can cut through. In Ephesians 6, Paul refers to the shield of faith, stopping the fiery arrows of the evil one. All the full armor, an allegorical image likened to the highest, most resistant body armor of the day, indicates protection to stand and not even take hits. John writes *"...and this is the victory that has overcome the world—our faith"* (1 John 5:4).

Several years ago, Barbara and I were doing an extended conference overseas with 4,000 people for nine days. What an honor it was, and so incredibly orderly!

At the closing of one of the evening meetings I had an unforgettable power encounter. I was walking toward the back of the tent, and over 100 people on both sides of the tent began snarling and shrieking, their contorted bodies manifesting demonic activity. I was shocked by the sudden outburst; I'd have to be here for weeks to help all these folks! Then something rose up from within me—an eruption of faith. With a loud voice I said, "Stop it and shut up!" They fell silent in a heap like dead bodies. I then commanded the demons out of them and the region, to go before God for His dispersion. I spoke blessing, healing, and comfort over them. To my amazement they arose free, worshiping the Lord and filled with His Spirit.

The authority and power of the Kingdom is awesome and humbling. It is "faith working through love" that wields protected, victorious engagement (Gal. 5:6). You see, love never fails; all the leaders, workers, and intercessors were there for the love of God. We had just closed with the sweetest worship, and He was giving those demons a nervous breakdown. I was just one shield-of-faith guy standing with an army of "faith working through love" warriors. Together we are a fortress.

GREATER IS HE

Heaven's strategies do not always seem logical, but we have to push past our unbelief and buy into God's plan. He will always give us enough information to recharge our faith, which will permit us to cooperate with His plan.

One of the best examples of this in the Bible is the familiar story of Elisha and the mighty Syrian army (see 2 Kings 6:8-23). The king of Syria had been fighting against Israel, but his plans were continually being foiled by prophetic words from Elisha, who (according to a Syrian informant) *"tells the king of Israel the words that you speak in your bedroom"* (2 Kings 6:12).

The king of Syria took his army and trapped Elisha in the city where he lived. When Elisha's servant saw their city surrounded with horses and chariots, he was petrified. But Elisha reassured him, *"Do not fear, for those who are with us are more than those who are with them"* (2 Kings 6:16). Then Elisha prayed, asking the Lord to open his servant's eyes. Suddenly the young man could see the entire mountainside thronging with a heavenly army, complete with chariots of fire.

Subsequently, Elisha asked God to strike the Syrians blind, which He did, and then Elisha misled them to follow him right into the heart of Samaria. Even then, God's warfare strategy was unusual. Instead of striking the Syrian soldiers down, Elisha advised the king of Israel to give them food and drink and then to send them back to their own king. This caused the Syrian raids to cease for the time being.

A little while later, Elisha found himself in the middle of another conflict, and again he brought a prophetic word of the Lord to announce God's unorthodox rescue strategy. The city of Samaria had been held under a military siege for so long that the people were reduced to eating dove's dung and donkey heads and even their own babies (see 2 Kings 6:24-33; 7:1-19). The king summoned Elisha, and he delivered this improbable-sounding word:

> *"About this time tomorrow, a seah of flour shall be sold for a shekel, and two seahs of barley for a shekel, at the gate of Samaria." The officer on whose arm the king was leaning*

said to the man of God, "Look, even if the Lord should open the floodgates of the heavens, could this happen?" "You will see it with your own eyes," answered Elisha, "but you will not eat any of it!" (2 Kings 7:1-2 NIV)

This is where God's strategy begins to unfold. Four lepers, who were living as outcasts outside the city walls, became the heroes of the story. They were beggars, and the siege had reduced them to skin and bones. With certain death facing them either way, they decided to head out toward the enemy camp to beg there.

But when they arrived at the edge of the Aramean camp, they found it deserted. God had caused the soldiers to hear the sound of chariots and horses, which had convinced them that the Samaritan king must have found foreign allies to come to his assistance. Terrified, the entire army fled in disarray.

The incredulous lepers found tables already set and food already cooked. They had never seen so much wealth in their lives! They gorged themselves and helped themselves to clothing and other plunder, and then they woke up to the fact that the desperate people of the besieged city needed to know what had just happened. So they notified the gatekeepers, and the people rushed out to share in the spoil.

In their haste, they trampled to death the officer who had mocked Elisha. So it was true that within less than 24 hours, flour and barley were again available in the market for ordinary prices, and Elisha's word about the officer not eating any of it was also true.

If God can use four lepers to fulfill a seemingly impossible prophecy to reverse horrific circumstances within less than 24 hours, why cannot He use any humble servant today? An army of angels awaits God's command at all times, and God wants to reveal and demonstrate His strength just as much now as He did then.

BLESSINGS INSTEAD OF CURSES

Some months, I fly coast-to-coast every week. This is a huge country. I look out the windows as I fly over the United States of America and I speak blessings over the rivers, the valleys, the cities, the empty places. I believe that God wants to pour out blessings on people and the world He has created. The mercy of God triumphs over judgment. One word from Him drives out darkness from our minds and the places we go.

God's words carry glorious light into dark places, and they invade every aspect of life. But somebody must hear what He's saying and carry His words into those places. Somebody—you and I and the believers we know—must learn to understand the subtleties in His voice as we tune out the distractions that our defeated foe throws at us.

Like the national bird, the bald eagle, we do not have to use our own strength to soar. We can learn how to sense the updraft of God's Spirit so we can wheel and circle long and high. Borne along on the wind, we can stop trying to get ahead of everything. We can just rest on His invisible power as we scan the world below. It looks a lot different from up there. Our perspective is greatly improved. With our sharp eagle-vision, we can see the smallest details in the great reaches of earth and sky.

Your spirit communes with His. His angels soar with you. Sometimes in unison, you cry out a single word or two from time to time. You were born for this!

> *From the rising of the sun to its going down the Lord's name is to be praised. The Lord is high above all nations, His glory above the heavens. …Blessed be the name of the Lord from this time forth and forevermore!* (Psalm 113:3-4,2)

Chapter 10

Nets for the Harvest
James W. Goll

An unexpected miracle occurred after Jesus' death and resurrection, when He manifested Himself to several of His disciples:

After these things Jesus showed Himself again to the disciples at the Sea of Tiberias, and in this way He showed Himself: Simon Peter, Thomas called the Twin, Nathanael of Cana in Galilee, the sons of Zebedee, and two others of His disciples were together. Simon Peter said to them, "I am going fishing." They said to him, "We are going with you also." They went out and immediately got into the boat, and that night they caught nothing. But when the morning had now come, Jesus stood on the shore; yet the disciples did not know that it was Jesus. Then Jesus said to them, "Children, have you any food?" They answered Him, "No." And He said to them, "Cast the net on the right side of the boat, and you will find some." So they cast, and now they were not able to draw it in because of the multitude of fish. Therefore that disciple whom Jesus loved said to Peter, "It is the Lord!" Now when Simon Peter heard that it was the Lord, he put on his outer garment (for he had removed it), and plunged into the sea. But the other disciples came in the little boat (for they were not far from land, but about two hundred cubits), dragging the net with fish. Then, as soon as they had come to land, they saw a fire of coals there, and fish laid on it, and bread. Jesus said to them, "Bring some of the fish which you have just caught." Simon Peter went up and dragged the net to land, full of large fish, one hundred and fifty-three; and although there were so many, the net was not broken (John 21:1-11).

We need the same miracle today—we need Yeshua, Jesus the resurrected Messiah, to manifest Himself again to those of us who are His disciples. We need Him to tell us to cast our nets on the other side of our boats, because we have been trying to catch fish all night long, and even though we thought we knew what we were doing we have not caught a thing. We need Him to shake things up and change the rules. We need Him to do what we cannot do by ourselves.

With Jesus on the scene, things happen. When He is missing, you cannot do anything to make up for it. You can paint your boat a different color; you can get a bigger anchor; you can get a bigger sail; you can even have a motor on your boat. But without His specific, on-the-spot instructions, your work will be in vain.

DO YOU HAVE ANY FISH?

If Jesus asked you, "Do you have any fish?" what would be your answer? For many of us, the answer would be no. We have toiled through the long dark hours, and we have nothing to show for it. If only Jesus would give us new assignments, fresh orders, new mandates for the challenging times in which we live.

A better question might be, "Do you have any *new* fish?" because the Church still seems to be cooking the ones left over from 20 years ago, swapping fish from church to church, not really growing, merely transferring the "catch" from one net to another. It's kind of like playing the "shell game"—we keep hiding the same peanut under different shells and each new guy calls it "church growth." I think we can do better than that!

The only way to haul in a new catch is by miraculous means. We need to know when, where, and how to deploy our nets, and only the Lord Jesus can give us that revelatory information. We would hope that those of us who are close to Jesus' heart (as was John the Beloved) will be the first ones who recognize Him when He shows up in the dim light of early dawn. "It is the Lord" may be all we need to say.

Then those of us who are more like Peter, poised for action, can grab our traveling clothes and plunge in. After a long time of waiting, stripped for work, we will be "mantled" with new authority so that we can throw ourselves into the sea of God's purposeful presence. As Peter swam to shore eagerly, the other disciples came along in their little boat. (God bless all the "little boats" out there. We need the ocean liners, but more than that, we need all of the faithful little boats.) Peter was already on shore talking to Jesus as they maneuvered the little boat slowly toward shore, dragging the huge catch of fish along. Somehow, even before they got there with their full net, Jesus was cooking some fish over a charcoal fire. (I wonder where He got His fish? He is always going before and preparing the way ahead of time.)

CASTING YOUR NET ON THE OTHER SIDE

After laboring all night without sleep, the disciples were weary. When the man on the shore told them to cast their net on the right side of the boat, they could have argued, "But that does not make any sense; we have not caught a single fish this whole night long." But they went ahead and did what He had suggested, not realizing until later that it was the all-knowing Creator of the universe who was instructing them.

The Lord Jesus will lend his revelatory insights to our empty-net situations as well. Our part is simply to obey to the best of our ability and to keep ourselves in position to obey some more. He may ask us to do some radical things. But if we follow His suggestions, full nets are guaranteed.

A few years ago, my youngest daughter, Rachel, persuaded me to go to a New Age fair to prophesy over people. I had heard about Christians doing such things, but I had never actually participated, so I went.

I sat down at this booth that Rachel's friends had set up. Along came a young man and he sat down in the chair on the outside of the table. The young woman who was directing the flow of the ministry at the booth started to explain to him, "Did you know that God still speaks today? He wants to tell us about our destiny…."

I started to get such a prophetic download for this guy that I could hardly stand it. I couldn't even stay on my side of the table. I broke the normal protocol, got up, walked around the table, and got down on my knees next to this young man, putting my arm around him like a father. I started weeping over this kid. He was 17 years old.

One of the high school students working at the booth, John, who was also 17 at the time, came around the end of the table, too, and he started ministering to this guy. He said, "Hey, listen, just pretend my voice is going to be the voice of Father God. God has something that He would like to say to you right now. First, would you forgive your own father for abandoning you and for not representing Me well?"

The kid began to weep, so now two of us were crying. He did not know God, although it was obvious that God was calling him. He did not know a thing about church. He said he was into Eckankar or something. He just kept on sobbing while John and the other kids in the booth were praying and speaking words of destiny over him.

Then he started manifesting demons; his arms started turning cold and blue, and it made our hair stand on end. I have been around deliverance ministry for so many years, I just said, "Oh, I know this one!" I just leaned in, letting the presence of Jesus inside me confront the demons. I addressed the demons one by one very quietly under my breath: "You come on out,

NETS FOR THE HARVEST

you spirit of rejection. Death wish, you come out in Jesus' name. Suicide, you come out...." I addressed several others, including witchcraft and the spirit of pharmacia (mind-altering drugs).

Gloriously delivered and free, this young guy was excited. So we led him in a "sinner's prayer" and he accepted Jesus right in the middle of the New Age fair. On top of that, we led him in a prayer to be baptized in the Holy Spirit. Swept up with a spirit of faith, I just said out loud to him, "Now speak!" Instantly, the Holy Spirit manifested Himself through him as a torrent of tongues came pouring out of his mouth.

Why am I telling about this experience? Because it shows what can happen when you obey Jesus' voice and cast your "net" in a different place. When I went to the New Age fair, I was casting my net on the other side of my boat at Jesus' suggestion, a side I hadn't tried yet. The results? A miraculous catch! I wonder who changed the most that day? I know I was radically impacted; never again do I want to return to my normal way of doing the prophetic. It was truly an adventure in the prophetic!

21 JUMP STREET

A couple of years ago, my friend Munday Martin and I, along with others, felt that God wanted us to initiate another unique "net-casting" venture. We starting setting aside the first three weeks of every August, encouraging people to "fast their comfort zones" and to join us in stepping outside our self-defined limits to hit the streets, looking for where the Spirit would have us spread a little supernatural love. We called our endeavor 21 Jump Street—taking Jesus to the streets—with a nod to the old television series, because we would be reaching the lost on the streets, bringing Martha and Mary together (see Luke 10:38-42). Research indicates that 21 days is the length of time required to develop a new habit. We wanted to allow enough time to develop new habits of listening to the Holy Spirit and obeying Him—wherever He might send us.

Over the next few years, people of all ages joined us, spurred on by Munday's ministry, Contagious Love International (http://www.contagiousloveintl.com), and our Encounters Network (http://www.encountersnetwork.com). We went to not only the city streets, but to the parks, schools, cafés, malls, movie theaters, hospitals, nursing homes, and wherever the Spirit led us.

What did we do? A variety of things, as the Spirit led us. We did prophetic evangelism (an informal version of what we did at the New Age fair); distributed food to the poor; servant evangelism, power evangelism, prayer for the sick, and evangelism through the arts; and we took praise bands to the streets. We reached out through block parties, dream interpretation booths in public areas, random acts of kindness, marketplace outreach, and more—doing whatever the Spirit told us to do.

Motivated by the Lord's words in Luke 14:21 (*"Go out quickly into the streets and lanes of the city, and bring in here the poor and the maimed and the lame and the blind"*), we encouraged each other to spread the Good News in whatever way His Spirit chose, even to the level of casting out demons, healing the sick, raising the dead, and moving in the supernatural power of God. We were aware of angels going with us and helping to bring about results.

Here is a report from Munday regarding one intriguing strategy for outreach:

> On a Friday, I led a team of around 12 people to a mall in Cleveland, Ohio. We all sat down together in the food court and waited on the Lord in small groups conducting a 'Treasure Hunt.' This is a very engaging group effort, which creates a real synergy in which everyone can be involved. We wait for clues from the Holy Spirit for people we will encounter, and even articles of clothing to look for, prior to even going. My team had the clues: (1) Fountain, (2) tie-dye, (3) and I got the name Kelly. Wouldn't you know it, our first encounter that day was when we found a fountain, two

children with tie-dye shirts standing nearby, and a mom. I felt led to approach the mom and I introduced myself, 'Hello, we are conducting a treasure hunt, and guess what, we have tie-dye and fountain as a clue.' Then I showed the mother our list with the name Kelly on it and asked if that pertained to her. With an excited look in her eyes she said that Kelly was her name! We got to plant the seed in her heart as Jesus gave us these clues for her and share with her that she was His treasure! This is so awesome![1]

Talk about casting your nets on the other side of the boat—or fountain, or mall!

As our nets were cast into new places, they did not come back empty. What an amazing adventure in the prophetic!

"Do the Double"

Jesus prophesied, *"I say to you, he who believes in Me, the works that I do he will do also; and greater works than these he will do, because I go to My Father"* (John 14:12). I call this "doing the double," and I believe that you and I are part of a generation that has been called to do these "greater works." By listening to the Holy Spirit and then casting our nets where He tells us to, we will be able to haul in a miraculous catch!

This generation, arising and breaking out of the box of traditional limitations, carries seven distinct characteristics:

1. Faith coupled with humility

2. An appreciation for working in teams (gender-inclusive)

3. Accountability with relational care, so that wounded warriors can be healed

4. An emphasis on the Fatherhood of God (not only the

revelation of Jesus the Son)

5. An ability to release the Holy Spirit with creativity (through the prophets and seers)

6. Increased power, clarity, and accuracy

7. An ability to see the target clearly

The Church is our practice ground but the world is our field of operations. As we come alongside each other to help each other hear and obey the voice of the Spirit, we will find ourselves doing far greater works than Jesus did while He was on earth, making it possible for His effectiveness to be multiplied as more territory becomes part of His Kingdom. Let His Kingdom come on earth as it is in Heaven!

PROPHETIC EVANGELISM

A simple term for "casting your nets on the other side of the boat" is *prophetic evangelism*, which simply means listening to the Spirit and acting accordingly to bring the Kingdom to bear on the world around you.

Prophetic evangelism combines the sustained emphasis on evangelism that was ushered in with the Reformation more than 600 years ago with the 100-plus-year emphasis on prophecy that began in 1904 when the Pentecostal outpouring occurred. As the earlier holiness movement shifted into the Pentecostal movement, which then shifted into the charismatic movement, the groundwork was laid for the current apostolic movement and beyond.

The priesthood of every believer makes it possible for the whole Church to be drawn into new realms of adventure with God. Prophetic evangelism has grown stronger as the Church has matured into a clearer understanding of her bridal intimacy with her Bridegroom, Jesus, along with the governmental empowerment (the "bridal rule") of God's people.

We are all to be prophetic evangelists, whether we find ourselves in megachurches and massive stadium events or in some back alley ministering to a homeless person; whether we end up as missionaries in the jungles of Colombia or in Starbucks holding a grande cup of Colombian coffee. The same Holy Spirit keeps speaking to us everywhere we go. He will link us up with others, equip us and teach us how to combine our gifts, and do signs and wonders through us. People will be unable to deny that this is God in action. The power, the love, and the unity will make Him manifest to a lost world.

A PROPHETIC PRAYER STORM

Foundational to prophetic evangelism—and breaking the way for its advance—is prophetic intercessory prayer. Another initiative of my own ministry has been what we call the Prayer Storm.

We have updated the 24/7 prayer model of the Moravians in Herrnhut, Germany, two centuries ago, establishing an Internet-based worldwide community of intercessors who commit to pray for one hour per week for revival in the church, a youth awakening, Israel, and God's intervention in times of crisis. This virtual house of prayer is storming the heavens even now, fueled by the responsiveness of the Spirit of God to the urgency of the times we live in.

With regular updates and reports, webcasts, and other resources, these prayer warriors are pioneering something that has never before been undertaken—blanketing the world with prophetic intercession around the clock that is not limited to one geographical spot.[2] We are restoring and re-releasing the global Moravian lamp stand, which is based on these words from the book of God's law: *"Fire shall be kept burning continually on the altar; it is not to go out"* (Lev. 6:13 NASB).

Throughout our intercession—not only in the Prayer Storm, but also at any other time—we must listen to the Holy Spirit. Without His ongoing guidance, we will soon flounder and falter. In concert with Him, we have the perseverance and energy and accuracy to keep praying until we see definite results.

When Jesus Gets into Your Boat

Prior to the Gospel account of the resurrected Jesus telling Peter and John and the other disciples to put their fishing net on the right side of the boat, we find another story about Jesus and His disciples in a fishing boat. This story gives us further insights into the adventure of prophetic discipleship:

> So it was, as the multitude pressed about Him to hear the word of God, that He stood by the Lake of Gennesaret, and saw two boats standing by the lake; but the fishermen had gone from them and were washing their nets. Then He got into one of the boats, which was Simon's, and asked him to put out a little from the land. And He sat down and taught the multitudes from the boat. When He had stopped speaking, He said to Simon, "Launch out into the deep and let down your nets for a catch." But Simon answered and said to Him, "Master, we have toiled all night and caught nothing; nevertheless at Your word I will let down the net." And when they had done this, they caught a great number of fish, and their net was breaking. So they signaled to their partners in the other boat to come and help them. And they came and filled both the boats, so that they began to sink. When Simon Peter saw it, he fell down at Jesus' knees, saying, "Depart from me, for I am a sinful man, O Lord!" For he and all who were with him were astonished at the catch of fish which they had taken; and so also were James and John, the sons of Zebedee, who were partners with Simon. And Jesus said to Simon, "Do not be afraid. From now on you will catch men." So when they had brought their boats to land, they forsook all and followed Him (Luke 5:1-11).

NETS FOR THE HARVEST

The questions this story raises in my mind are: (1) "What happens when Jesus steps into *your* boat?" and (2) "How can you get Him to step into your boat?"

Let's answer the second question first. Obviously, you must go to the water first. He will not get into your boat if it is stuck on dry land. Water, always strongly associated with the Holy Spirit, is where your boat needs to be floating. In other words, you have got to get into His presence.

Once you are out there on the water and in His presence, you need to know that Jesus is actually looking for a boat to step into. He looks out over the surface of the lake, scanning the vessels that have launched themselves away from the shore. He sees more than one boat, but He does not get into each one of them in turn. He looks for the right boat, the one that is ready for Him. Jesus is personal. As we read about Him in the book of Revelation:

> *Behold, I stand at the door and knock. If anyone hears My voice and opens the door, I will come in to him and dine with him, and he with Me* (Revelation 3:20).

Jesus checks out the boats, sees the one He wants, and invites Himself aboard. When He looks in your direction, will you say yes to Him? Knowing that your life may change drastically as a result, will you accept His invitation? If He follows His own example, He will get into only one of the boats that He sees. Just one. Will it be yours?

When Jesus gets into a boat, He does it because He has something to say. So if He gets into someone *else's* boat, regardless of how you feel personally, you need to bless that person (or church or city) and the word that the Lord Jesus will be bringing them. If He does get into your boat—listen to Him! He may bring a word of correction, clarification, or direction. He may ask you to do something that is beyond your abilities. In fact, you can just about count on it; that's one of the ways you can tell it's the Holy Spirit speaking. He will say something like, "Launch out into the deep and let down your nets for a catch."

He will tell you to do something that seems a little eccentric or extreme, something that you may have tried already without results. "But Master, we have toiled all night and caught nothing…." Still, you will recognize the voice of God's authority and you will agree: "… nevertheless at Your word I will let down the net." The results will prove that you have the Lord in your boat.

In response to your own miraculous catch, will you do what Simon Peter did? He fell down at Jesus' feet, humbled and awed, completely aware that he did not deserve this phenomenal miracle, and willing to change in any way that the Lord might require. When the Lord Jesus steps into your boat, His presence brings you to your knees. Your response will be humility—and change.

When He gets into your boat, it will cost you your boat, your history, and everything you own. What happened to Peter and the others? The catch of fish was so great that they had to have help bringing it in. They brought their overloaded boats to shore, only to drop everything and follow Jesus. No longer would they be known as the fishermen from Lake Gennesaret. Now the whole world would be their place of work, and they would follow the voice of their Lord wherever He would lead them.

Their miraculous catch of fish? They shared it with the other fishermen, blessing them instead of hanging onto the blessing for themselves.

A Messenger with a Message

With that one miracle and their response to it, Simon Peter and his partners, James and John, changed overnight. They went from ordinary fishermen who spent their time and energy toiling to earn a living to messengers with a message, a Kingdom message. From that time forward, they would have something to say, and their voices would be heard.

In the same way, when Jesus steps into your boat and changes your life, He will give you a message. You will become a messenger. Far from being a lone voice in the wilderness, your voice will join the voices of other

Kingdom messengers. You will enjoy a spiritual synergy and a supernatural convergence with other messengers past and present. You will not be able to claim credit for anything except for having said yes to your assignment and your Lord.

Now He can use you as never before. His blessings will take many forms, and you will hang in there with Him even when the going gets tough. You will go where He goes and do what He tells you to do, living a supernaturally natural life in relationship with Him. Walking down the road together—or back on the water in a boat together—your conversations will revolve around the things that are on His heart.

Passionate because He is passionate, you will enjoy your journey in the company of His Spirit. Gifted with the prophetic ability to hear Him even when you cannot see Him, you, too, will embark upon an endless exploration of the diverse challenges of helping to bring in His Kingdom where darkness once prevailed. This is the purpose of these amazing giftings of the Holy Spirit. This is the power of the Gospel of the Kingdom of our dear Lord Jesus Christ.

Let the adventure begin!

ENDNOTES

1. Munday Martin, Contagious Love International, as reported to James Goll on August 14, 2009. Archived at http://www.ministrytothenations.org/email_archive.html.

2. For more information about Prayer Storm, see www.prayerstorm.com. You can join the Prayer Storm—"the hour that changes the world"—and help restore global presence evangelism and the great revivals of the past.

Epilogue

PROPHETIC DIVERSITY
James W. Goll

Anna was a prophetess:

> *Now there was one, Anna, a prophetess, the daughter of Pha-*
> *nuel, of the tribe of Asher. She was of a great age, and had*
> *lived with a husband seven years from her virginity; and this*
> *woman was a widow of about eighty-four years, who did not*
> *depart from the temple, but served God with fastings and*
> *prayers night and day. And coming in that instant she gave*
> *thanks to the Lord, and spoke of Him to all those who looked*
> *for redemption in Jerusalem* (Luke 2:36-38).

She is only mentioned this one time in the Bible. We do not have a record of one single prophecy she ever uttered. But this passage does say that she talked about the coming Messiah constantly. And when Mary and Joseph brought the baby Jesus into the temple, she recognized Him as the One who was coming to redeem Israel. She knew who He was, even though He was just a little baby. He was the One she had been waiting for.

The authenticity of her prophetic gift was proven, not so much by that moment in the Temple as it was by the way she had always been talking about Him. The words of a true prophet point to Jesus, the beloved Son of God.

I would love for it to be said of me that I was "like Anna," someone who focused on nothing and nobody except Jesus. In every prophetic word, long ones or short ones; every vision; every dream; every inspired prayer, I want to be declaring the testimony of Jesus (see Rev. 19:10). I want to be like John the Beloved, leaning my head on His chest and then telling others about Him.

Do you love Him? If you love Him, your heart will overflow with words about Him:

> *My heart is overflowing with a good theme; I recite my composition concerning the King; my tongue is the pen of a ready writer. You are fairer than the sons of men; grace is poured upon Your lips; therefore God has blessed You forever* (Psalm 45:1-2).

In loving Him, none of us will be exactly like Anna because the overflow will take different forms. The message of love will come in different wrappings, and it will be presented in different styles. Marketplace manners are a little different from prophetic conferences. Culture differs from place to place.

But the simple truth is that all adventures in the prophetic realm must be rooted in the same soil—expressing the love of God.

SHOWING HOW MUCH GOD LOVES SOMEONE ELSE

The prophetic gift helps us understand how much God loves us personally. But as the gift operates upon, in, and through you, it becomes a demonstration of how much God loves someone else.

When you stir up the gift and release it, you are doing what the apostle Paul taught: *"Pursue love, and desire spiritual gifts, but especially that you may prophesy"* (1 Cor. 14:1). Prophecy in its pure form is supposed to be about loving people with Jesus' love. God has put into you a tiny measure of His massive heart of love, and His Spirit decides to open up a little spigot. Even a tiny measure of His love overwhelms us, whether it comes with amazing signs and wonders or in the midst of a calm, little conversation. Regardless of the delivery system, a true prophetic word communicates the life-giving love of God to another human heart.

For each of us, the various expressions of the prophetic gift differ depending on our personalities and what God has called us to. Each of us is a unique creature. No two people are the same. God never uses a cookie cutter. The varieties of giftings and ministries that we read about in the New Testament become further varied as they are expressed through such a wide variety of individuals. And yet He Himself never changes.

> There are diversities of gifts, but the same Spirit. There are differences of ministries, but the same Lord. And there are diversities of activities, but it is the same God who works all in all (1 Corinthians 12:4-6).

RELEVANT SHIFTS

Besides the differences in personalities and in applications of the prophetic gifts, I am continually noticing additional diversity in the prophetic realm. Within the body of Christ, we are finding a wider ethnic diversity than ever before, and we are also hearing fresh voices. Even more new voices are just over the horizon. Most of them are young, but not all of them.

We are hearing new prophetic sounds in terms of up-to-the-minute media presentations. Continuous change seems to be the new norm. We are trying new things and figuring out what works best. New ways of thinking require flexibility and adjustment. From prophetic evangelism at New Age fairs to solemn assemblies of hungry, passionate young people, the name of Jesus is being proclaimed as never before.

Other relevant shifts include new aims and goals. I call it the gutter and the gold. No longer can the prophetic movement be at home only in middle class churches. As the Spirit leads, the prophetic is finding its way into hopeless slums and secularized governmental offices.

Year after year, new models of Kingdom life are developing. They include everything from mega-churches to small house churches, from crowded stadiums to widely dispersed webcasts. Some flourish in places that have become centers of spiritual life, while others remain hidden from the public eye. Such a wide variety of new possibilities abound in this shifting prophetic landscape that I have tried to capture them in a *memorable* way. Here are my "Nine Ms":

1. *Mighty* streams of prayer and praise, combined with the prophetic, are encouraging the *manifest presence* of God. The worship movement is maturing and bringing us into higher realms of glory.

2. *Miracle manifestations* are proliferating, not only in Third World countries, but also in the West.

3. *Marketplace ministry*, never heard of until recently, is increasing. Guided by the Holy Spirit, Christians exercise their prophetic gifts in their places of secular employment, bringing much-needed wisdom and prophetic intercession into new situations.

4. The *matrix* of relationships. The gifts do not thrive in isolation; they require a healthy relational community of faith.

5. *Missions* outreach. In spite of world recession and the well-established indigenous Church, both long-term and short-term missions continue to be launched, based in many countries including places that until recently were on the receiving end of missionary activity.

6. *Middle East* emphasis: God is doing something in Israel and in the regions surrounding Israel as people bring the gospel of the Kingdom to the Jew first and them to the Gentile (see Rom. 1:16).

7. *Ministry* training. With the proliferation of ministry training centers and the organic spreading of the mentoring movement, established prophets, pastors, and teachers are able to give away what they have earned and learned. People are realizing that the little bit they have may be someone else's magnificent meal.

8. *Mercy ministries.* My wife responded to a call for this one. She ministered in Mozambique, Thailand, among the First Nations people, and wherever else she was able, and she called it "the poor man's watch." In fact, she purchased a cheap watch for one of those trips, thinking that she would give it away to someone who needed it. When she came home, she still had it on, and she felt that God was using it to remind her that she was on a prophetic mission to the poor, a true poor man's (prayer) watch.

9. *Media mania* (I'm just reaching for more "Ms"!)—another way of saying that every new means of communication, public and private, is being used by people of the Kingdom.

Although we differ theologically and in many other ways, the Holy Spirit is helping the worldwide Church to achieve a remarkable level of unity and energy in "doing the stuff," as John Wimber used to say. Whether we face more storms or times of fulfillment, it is time to seize the moment, listening to the Spirit for direction. The Body of Christ is accepting an incredible opportunity to shift and move into Kingdom alignment. This is one of the reasons this book has been written—so that you, too, can find your place in this amazing adventure.

GETTING IT TOGETHER

I wish personal character could have been an outright gift of the Spirit like the gift of prophecy or the word of wisdom. Our character flaws contribute more to our ministry failures than any other factor. And yet bequeathing us such puny character represents a stroke of genius on the part of God, who wants us to rely on Him for everything.

Here He is, living inside each person who names Him as Lord, with a goal of transforming us into His image day by day. As we come into union with the Creator of the universe, who knows us better than we will ever know ourselves, we grow in our experience of new creation realities. Christ in us is the hope of glory (see Col. 1:27).

The Spirit who dwells inside us is also the spirit of prophecy, and, as you will remember, the spirit of prophecy is the testimony of Jesus (see Rev. 19:10). As the spirit of prophecy draws you continually to the Lord of Love, you will know God better and better. As John the Beloved, the one who leaned his head on Jesus' heart, put it:

> *This is the message which we have heard from Him and declare to you, that God is light and in Him is no darkness at all. If we say that we have fellowship with Him, and walk in darkness, we lie and do not practice the truth. But if we walk in the light as He is in the light, we have fellowship with one another, and the blood of Jesus Christ His Son cleanses us from all sin* (1 John 1:5-7).

There is our cure for weak character and our primary prophetic message. What an adventure this life with Him is turning out to be! We are part of the generation that walks in "the double"—fullness of fruit (character) and fullness of power (gifts of the Holy Spirit). When we add the fullness of the Spirit of wisdom to the mix—oh, what an adventure that will truly be!

THE CONTRIBUTING AUTHORS

DR. JAMES W. GOLL is the president of Encounters Network, director of Prayer Storm, and coordinates Encounters Alliance, a coalition of leaders. He has shared Jesus in more than 40 nations and has authored numerous books including *The Seer*, *Dream Language,* and *Angelic Encounters.* James and Michal Ann were married for over 32 years until her graduation into Heaven in the fall of 2008. Together they had four children. Visit www.encountersnetwork.com and www.prayerstorm.com for more information.

MICHAL ANN GOLL was the founder of Compassion Acts and the co-founder of Encounters Network with her husband, James. She ministered worldwide and was known for her compassion for others and her passion for Jesus. She was the author of the trilogy *Women on the Frontlines* and the newly published *Empowered Women* in her honor. James and Michal Ann were married for over 32 years until her graduation into Heaven in September 2008. They have four wonderful adult children who carry on her legacy in Christ. Visit www.compassionacts.com for more information.

After surviving a "death's door" experience and spiritual rebirth, for the past 30 years, **Mickey Robinson** has had a public speaking ministry releasing hope and the prophetic gifts. Mickey also serves as a director of Prophetic Christian Ministries Association, president of the Lazarus Foundation (a care and discipleship center for the physically challenged), and Seagate Ministries. Mickey and his wife, Barbara, their four children, and four grandchildren live in Franklin, Tennessee. To learn more, visit www.mickeyrobinson.com.

Jeff Jansen, founder of Global Fire Ministries, is a revivalist whose ministry of faith, power, and revelation has affected countless lives. Jeff ministers in churches, conferences, and crusades throughout the nations where he openly preaches the Gospel of the Kingdom with explosive supernatural demonstrations of signs, wonders, miracles, and other manifestations in the Glory. Jeff, Jan, and their family have all made their homes in middle Tennessee throughout the Nashville area. To learn more, visit www.globalfireministries.org.

Ryan Wyatt is the founder and apostolic team leader of Abiding Glory Ministries, which incorporates the Abiding Glory International Ministry Base and The Habitation (their local fellowship of believers), both headquartered in Knoxville, Tennessee. Ryan, his wife Kelly, and their three sons live in Knoxville. To learn more, visit www.abidingglory.com.

Patricia King is president of both Extreme Prophetic and Christian Services Association. She has been a pioneering voice in ministry with over 30 years of background as a Christian minister in conference speaking, prophetic service, church leadership, and television and radio appearances. Patricia has written numerous books, produced many CDs and DVDs, hosts Extreme Prophetic Television, and is the CEO of a popular online media network—XPmedia.com. Patricia's reputation in the Christian community is world-renowned. To learn more, visit www.xpmedia.com.

REFLECTIONS